Synthesis Lectures on Technology and Health

The series publishes state-of-the-art short books on transformative technologies for health, wellness, and independent living. Our scope of publishing in the expanding health tech field includes:

- Technology in support of active and healthy living and aging
- Digital technologies for health- and social-care improvement
- Diagnostic, screening, and tracking tools
- Assistive and rehabilitative technologies

The series includes a subseries of books published in partnership with Canada's AGE-WELL that specifically addresses their 8 AgeTech Challenge Areas. Each lecture introduces the context in which the technology is used—wellness, health, medicine, special needs, or other contexts. Authors present and explain the technology and review promising applications and opportunities as well as limitations and challenges. They include material on their own work while surveying the broader landscape of related research, development, and impact.

Deborah Fels · Shital Desai · Margot Whitfield ·
Peter Pennefather · Evan Hibbard

Inclusive Design Premises, Policies, Protocols, and Practices: From Usability to Empowerment

Springer

Deborah Fels
Ted Rogers School of Information Technology Management
Inclusive Media and Design Centre
Toronto Metropolitan University
Toronto, ON, Canada

Margot Whitfield
Faculty of Information
University of Toronto
Toronto, ON, Canada

Evan Hibbard
Faculty of American Sign Languages and Deaf Studies
California State University
Sacramento, CA, USA

Shital Desai
School of Arts, Media, Performance and Design
York University
Toronto, ON, Canada

Peter Pennefather
Leslie Dan Faculty of Pharmacy
University of Toronto
Toronto, ON, Canada

ISSN 2771-7054 ISSN 2771-7070 (electronic)
Synthesis Lectures on Technology and Health
ISBN 978-3-032-15745-4 ISBN 978-3-032-15746-1 (eBook)
https://doi.org/10.1007/978-3-032-15746-1

This Springer imprint is published by the registered company Springer Nature Switzerland AG
The registered company address is: Gewerbestrasse 11, 6330 Cham, Switzerland

The authors would like to dedicate this book to all the students with disabilities that have inspired us to write about our experiences in the hopes that others will benefit.

Acknowledgements

The authors would like to thank Ron Baecker for his never-ending patience and assistant. This book would not have happened without his support and encouragement. We would also like to thank the reviewers for their insight and wisdom about this important subject. Finally, we would like to thank the editors at Springer who helped make this book possible.

AGE-WELL (www.agewell-nce.ca) is Canada's Technology and Aging Network. The pan-Canadian network brings together researchers, older adults, caregivers, partner organizations, and future leaders to accelerate the delivery of technology-based solutions that make a meaningful difference in the lives of Canadians. AGE-WELL researchers are producing technologies, services, policies, and practices that improve quality of life for older adults and caregivers and generate social and economic benefits for Canada. AGE-WELL's work is supported through Government of Canada funding programs.

The Science and Technology for Aging Research (STAR) Institute (www.sfu.ca/starinstitute) at Simon Fraser University (SFU) is committed to supporting community-engaged research in the rapidly growing area of technology and aging. The Institute supports the development and implementation of technologies to address many of the health challenges encountered in old age, as well as addresses the social, commercial, and policy aspects of using and accessing technologies. STAR also supports the AGE-WELL network.

AGEWELL

STAR INSTITUTE
Science and Technology for Aging Research
Simon Fraser University

Contents

About the Authors

Deborah Fels, P.Eng., Ph.D. (1994) Professor at Toronto Metropolitan University, has over 35 years of experience in the areas of Inclusive Design, Human Factors, and Human–Computer Interaction with a specific focus on designing, developing and evaluating technologies for people with disabilities. Her research interests involve inclusive design, access to media and technology for people with disabilities, and inclusive business. She has published over 190 articles and received three patents.

Shital Desai, Ph.D. is Associate Professor of Interaction Design in the School of Arts, Media, Performance and Design and the York Research Chair in Accessible Interaction Design at York University. Her work examines how emerging technologies such as XR and AI can support everyday activities, communication, and relational closeness by understanding people's needs, habits, and rituals and by adapting to these dynamic contexts of use. She has published over 35 articles.

Margot Whitfield, MMSt is Researcher and Accessibility Consultant dedicated to advancing inclusive access to arts, culture, and information. A Master's student at the University of Toronto, her interest in human factors and critical disability theory stems from a decade of user studies with blind, Deaf, wheelchair users and neurodivergent participants. She has co-authored 11 publications.

Peter Pennefather, Ph.D. Professor Emeritus, University of Toronto, has over 40 years' expertise in neuroscience, cellular biophysics, and data science. In recent years his scholarly activities have focused on the need for and utility of authenticating and qualifying data values. He has published over 130 articles. He is also President of gDial Inc, which holds several patents on technical solutions for generating self-referencing, self-authenticating data files.

Evan Hibbard, Ph.D. is Deaf Academic and Accessibility Advocate with over 20 years of diverse teaching experience. He co-founded the Deaf, Crip, Mad Faculty and Staff employee resource group at California State University, Sacramento. Born Deaf and culturally Deaf, he is active in Deaf communities and advises Deaf graduate students and their professors on strategies for building inclusive graduate-level learning environments. His research explores Deaf media, accessibility, captioning and online teaching to identify issues for Deaf and disabled users.

List of Figures

List of Tables

1 Introduction

There is a need for many human perspectives in design processes as design is for people and people are multifaceted (Dreyfuss 2003). Conventional practices do not necessarily account for the diversity of perspectives. User-Centred Design and Inclusive Design are often considered together where one is the umbrella of the other or vice versa (Persson et al. 2015). In this book, we are considering Inclusive Design as the design framework that encompasses the principles of User-Centred Design (see Appendix).

1.1 Inclusive Human-Centred Design

Computing environments have emerged from the industrial era, shaped by imperatives of productivity and conformity, proliferating in intelligence and penetrating all aspects of people's everyday lives. However, many of these systems have been designed and developed based on mechanical principles of stimuli and response. These methods of development have often been harmful in their widespread disabling practices and further stigmatisation of human diversity, particularly those at the margins, including people with disabilities. People with disabilities (PWD), a classification system for tool development that further compartmentalises and reduces individuals to their functional differences, whether they be cognitive (neurodivergent), physical, mental or perceivable, rather than categorized by similarities (e.g. humanness) or through other means, such as culture. Some PWD have reclaimed cultural and linguistic identities from these original medically oriented definitions. For example, instead of the term Deaf referring to some specific level of hearing loss, it relates to individuals who use a visual-spatial language(s) to communicate, and experience shared cultural and social values as a result. People who

D. Fels et al., *Inclusive Design Premises, Policies, Protocols, and Practices: From Usability to Empowerment*, Synthesis Lectures on Technology and Health,
https://doi.org/10.1007/978-3-032-15746-1_1

are Deaf and PWD may not self-identify with a disability for fear of stigma, particularly those with hidden or mental disabilities, such as bipolar and depression.

Able-bodied/neurotypical and PWD/neurodivergent alike are expected to adapt to and learn about the computing environment based on mechanistic principles (e.g., Dijksterhuis 1961; Lakoff and Johnson 2008) which are built to the exclusion of PWD. Accommodations then are tools to modify disabling computer and education environments. They include use of support technology, such as screen readers, virtual attendance technologies, personnel (such as note takers) or spoken language-signed language interpreters (called interpreters in this book but, may also be referred to as intervenors, particularly in the case of Deaf/Blind users).

Inclusive Design as a model or theory of design arose in the 1990s in the United Kingdom (UK). It originated as a designer-focused framework driven by access to services as well as built environments and products for PWD (Imrie and Hall 2003). Other models, such as Universal Design (Null 2013; Ostroff 2011; Steinfeld and Maisel 2012), originating in the United States, or Design for All (Bendixen and Benktzon 2015; Ruiz et al. 2011; Stephanidis 2021), originating in Europe, preceded Inclusive Design and were originally driven by the need to access built environments or access to information and communication technologies respectively (Clarkson et al. 2003). Regardless, these models have similar constructs to Inclusive Design with some variations. In this book, Inclusive Design is the model used to frame the discussion and applications in each chapter. We suggest that it is not a trend or fad but an enduring design approach that encompasses and enables the diversity and differing abilities of human populations.

As a brief introduction to the tenets of Inclusive Design, Clarkson et al. (2003) suggests that Inclusive Design is where "designers ensure that their products and services address the needs of the widest possible audience, irrespective of age or ability," (p. 235). While this is a very broad definition, others have provided further tenets to further and clarify this broad concept. For example, (Developing BS7000 Part 6—Guide to Managing Inclusive Design 2004) added that one product or service cannot necessarily meet the needs of "all" individuals or abilities and Treviranus (2024) suggested that specialized products designed for particular individual or groups is not an efficient or cost-effective approach. Regardless of the origins and adoptions of the original theoretical tenets, further development of the concept has evolved from varying perspectives. Combined this includes consideration for:

1. Introducing Inclusive Design at the beginning of a product, environment or service development decision-making process or lifecycle, rather than at the end. This includes anticipating user needs, preferences and abilities proactively;
2. Customizability or "one-size-fits-one" (Treviranus 2010) where products and services are adaptable or can be modified to meet specific users' ongoing or changing needs. For example, as children grow, their educational needs change.

(a) Diversity of needs are not restricted to disability but also relates to culture, gender, age, lifestyle, location of use (e.g., at home, at work) and environmental conditions (e.g., weather, social, public versus private) considerations or preferences (Waller et al. 2015).
(b) Equity rather than equality (Minow 2021; Zallio and Clarkson 2021)
3. Collaborating and evaluating with a diverse range of users and stakeholders from the beginning of the process as co-designers, team members, advisors, and evaluators (Cappelen and Andersson 2021; Fuglerud et al. 2020; Inclusive Design Research Centre n.d.) using inclusive methods.
4. The business case where designing businesses and business processes can incorporate inclusion (Clarkson et al. 2003); and
5. Policy development—where inclusive design can inform government or industry regulations and policies for product, environment or service development and deployment, as well as, purchasing requirements for government or industry (Shogren et al. 2021).

While these constructs are useful and informative for defining the Inclusive Design model, it can be difficult for researchers, designers, business owners, directors, or others to implement them. First, it can be very difficult to understand or know all possible types of users, and their needs and preferences, particularly for novices. It is also difficult not to draw on personal experience only; for example, a researcher's experience in interacting with her grandmother who is living with dementia is the only context that informs the researcher's development of an online tool for diagnosing dementia. Instead, collaborating with people living with a dementia diagnosis means including them in research activities and team meetings as co-designers or co-researchers, and involving them in formative and summative evaluation sessions. Invested community partners, such as hospitals and care homes, community centres, and formal and informal caregivers should also be included. Considerations for collaborating with invested partners is a common theme throughout this book and details of how to involve inclusive collaborations can be found in Chap. 3 (*Inclusive teaching*) *and* Chap. 4 (*Inclusive research methods*).

Keates and Clarkson (2003) developed the Inclusive Design Cube (see Fig. 1.1) as a way of characterizing user capabilities as low, medium or high in the mobility, sensory and cognitive dimensions. They recommend that designers, researchers, business owners, etc. consider the lowest level capabilities first (outermost region of the cube) before considering the higher levels. For example, a younger user who is neurodiverse may need sensory substitution (Alper 2018; McLean 2022) alternatives to visual and auditory displays, while an older user who is neurodiverse may have developed coping strategies to operate without these supports. Designing for the younger users in this example would take priority.

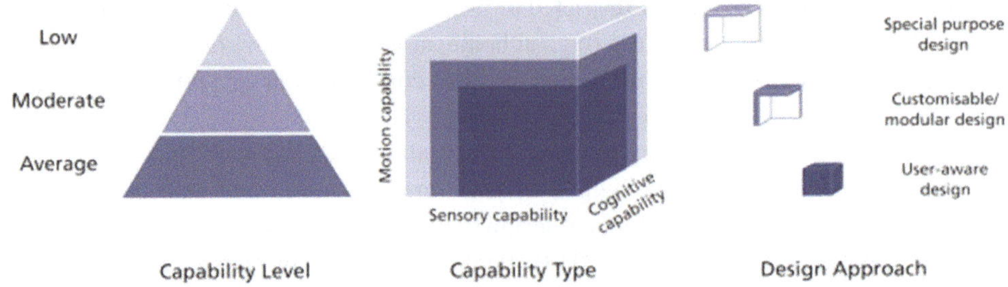

Fig. 1.1 Inclusive design cube (Clarkson and Coleman 2015 p. 236). Used with permission

1.2 Overview of Book

A policy argument for using an Inclusive Design approach to research, development and business relates to avoiding costly lawsuits if products and designs are considered inaccessible to specific populations and violate legislation or regulation on accessibility [e.g., Americans with Disabilities Act (Justice 2003) or the Accessible Canada Act (Branch 2019)]. Chapter 2 provides a brief overview of some different types of accessibility legislation, regulations and standards. For research, the equivalent criticism often relates to having insufficient participant numbers to be meaningful and generalizable, and thus are not worthy of consideration or publication.

Post-secondary educational institutions such as universities and colleges will often have services available to SWD for accessing educational resources and educational tasks such as materials, classroom spaces, test-taking, sign language interpretations and many others. Accommodation directives are provided to instructors who are required to abide by those directives without taking on the responsibility of creating an inclusive learning space. While training and information about being an inclusive instructor are available, they can be difficult to apply in a particular situation. In addition, teaching and graduate assistants who also participate in the learning and teaching settings are not necessarily part of the inclusive learning objectives. Chapter 3 introduces inclusive thinking for teaching and learning, and how to apply this thinking to create an inclusive learning environment for SWD. In particular, it challenges readers to consider time as a common denominator rather than the evaluation instrument, overt turn-taking mechanisms, the concepts of fairness and equity as applied to SWD.

Conducting user needs analyses, systematically analyzing products, services, environments, processes, and policies based on user capabilities, and having user and stakeholder collaborators, can aid in developing a designer's or researcher's knowledge and understanding of SWD. However, the methods for accomplishing these procedures are not necessarily accessible nor easy to use by the intended users or stakeholders. So, we have a quandary—how can user needs be assessed when the tools for conducting needs analyses are not inclusive? And, how do designers, researchers, business owners, and others know how to interact with a variety of users in order to understand their needs and preferences, or include them in the design and development processes? For example, how can a hearing designer learn how to facilitate a policy development meeting with a Deaf user when the nuances of Deaf culture go far beyond just employing a sign language interpreter?

In Chap. 4 on inclusive research methods, Sujan et al. (2017) use a similar approach as that used in the Inclusive Design Cube to characterize needs analysis methods by user capabilities. In this way, researchers, designers and others can determine which needs analysis method is better suited for their particular user population characteristics, or determine that an existing method should be revised.

Chapter 4 also provides description and discussion on mixed methods research that uses qualitative and quantitative methodologies in order to overcome concerns about small numbers and statistical analyses, and to elicit the diverse and rich ways PWD interact with the world. These data are necessary to provide designers, business and governments with the "how to" knowledge on being inclusive.

A common complaint about research and development efforts to include PWD is that populations are too small to justify investment of funding and resources. Inclusive Design argues that expenses can be reduced if a wide range of needs are considered from the beginning of the process. However, to do this requires knowledge and understanding of how to be an inclusive designer or developer, something that is neither taught at most educational institutions nor easy to learn. In addition, convincing business decision makers to embrace this approach requires Inclusive Design principles and practices to be converted into the language of business and strategy. Chapter 5 provides an Inclusive Design layer for a common business model, the Business Model Canvas, in order to assist in integrating Inclusive Design into the language and concepts of business. Finally, Chap. 6 outlines some of the considerations of inclusive design practices and implementation.

In summary, the main aim of this book is to provide a discussion, application and examples of how Inclusive Design can be considered and applied in business, research, and university level teaching. While there are numerous resources on Inclusive Design (e.g., *Web Content Accessibility Guidelines (WCAG) 2.1* n.d.; Langdon et al. 2012; Nicolaidis et al. 2019; Holloway and Barbareschi 2022; Buß 2020; Nicolle and Abascal 2001; Inclusive Design Research Centre n.d.; Joyce 2022), they tend to present a general perspective. This text is designed to assist researchers, instructors and business leaders to integrate Inclusive Design into their own practices. For this text, person first language is used to describe people. This usage is not general to all individuals, some individuals use person first language (National Network 2023), and others use identify-first language as in one of the authors of this chapter identifies as Deaf person. It is recommended to ask individuals their language preferences.

1.3 Limitations

The monograph does not present a comprehensive or in-depth analysis of theories or history of Inclusive Design as this requires a dedicated publication. However, it does present the basic premises of Inclusive Design and the convergence of them between different schools of thought. In addition, these premises are used as points of reference to underpin and justify the arguments presented in each chapter.

Examples are provided to illustrate and provide an applied perspective of the concepts discussed in each chapter. There are many other examples that could be equally valid and useful. Readers are challenged to seek alternative examples, particularly based on lived experience, that could also relate to the concepts presented.

Finally, this monograph does not present a comprehensive set of inclusive research or data analyses methods from either a theoretical or applied perspective. Inclusive research methods and data analyses are nascent and evolving areas. Much of the material contained in Chap. 4 is based on the author's own experiences over 35 years of attempting to develop and apply inclusive research methods, and qualitative and quantitative data analysis methods; there remains a long way to go. We hope that readers can take what is presented, extend the concepts and add to the literature in this area.

References

Alper, M. (2018). Inclusive sensory ethnography: Studying new media and neurodiversity in everyday life. *New Media & Society, 20*(10), 3560–3579.

Bendixen, K., & Benktzon, M. (2015). Design for All in Scandinavia–A strong concept. *Applied Ergonomics, 46*, 248–257.

Branch, L. S. (2019, July 11). *Consolidated federal laws of Canada, Accessible Canada Act*. https://laws-lois.justice.gc.ca/eng/acts/a-0.6/

Buß, R. (2020). Inclusive Design–Go Beyond Accessibility. *Human-Computer Interaction. Human Values and Quality of Life: Thematic Area, HCI 2020, Held as Part of the 22nd International Conference, HCII 2020, Copenhagen, Denmark, July 19–24, 2020, Proceedings, Part III 22*, 400–407.

Cappelen, B., & Andersson, A.-P. (2021). Trans-Create–Co-Design with Persons with Severe Disabilities. In *Universal Design 2021: From Special to Mainstream Solutions* (pp. 87–101). IOS Press.

Clarkson, P. J., & Coleman, R. (2015). History of inclusive design in the UK. *Applied Ergonomics, 46*, 235–247.

Clarkson, P. J., Coleman, R., Keates, S., & Lebbon, C. (2003). *Inclusive design: Design for the whole population*. Springer-Verlag.

Developing BS7000 Part 6—Guide to Managing Inclusive Design. (2004). In S. Keates, *Lecture Notes in Computer Science* (pp. 332–339). Springer Berlin Heidelberg. https://doi.org/10.1007/978-3-540-30111-0_29

Dijksterhuis, E. J. (1961). *The mechanization of the world picture* (Vol. 184). JSTOR.

Dreyfuss, H. (2003). *Designing for people*. Skyhorse Publishing Inc.

Fuglerud, K. S., Schulz, T., Janson, A. L., & Moen, A. (2020). Co-creating persona scenarios with diverse users enriching inclusive design. *Universal Access in Human-Computer Interaction. Design Approaches and Supporting Technologies: 14th International Conference, UAHCI 2020, Held as Part of the 22nd HCI International Conference, HCII 2020, Copenhagen, Denmark, July 19–24, 2020, Proceedings, Part I 22*, 48–59.

Holloway, C., & Barbareschi, G. (2022). *Disability Interactions: Creating Inclusive Innovations.* Springer International Publishing. https://doi.org/10.1007/978-3-031-03759-7

Imrie, R., & Hall, P. (2003). *Inclusive design: Designing and developing accessible environments.* Taylor & Francis.

Inclusive Design Research Centre. (n.d.-a). *Community-Led Co-design Kit.* Retrieved May 9, 2023, from https://co-design.inclusivedesign.ca/about/

Inclusive Design Research Centre. (n.d.b). *Welcome to The Inclusive Design Guide.* The Inclusive Design Guide. https://guide.inclusivedesign.ca/

Joyce, A. (2022, January 30). *Inclusive Design.* Nielsen Norman Group. https://www.nngroup.com/articles/inclusive-design/

Justice, U. D. of. (2003). *ADA home page* (Vol. 2003). http://www.usdoj.gov/crt/ada/adahom1.htm.

Keates, S., & Clarkson, P. J. (2003). Countering design exclusion: Bridging the gap between usability and accessibility. *Universal Access in the Information Society, 2*(3), Article 3.

Lakoff, G., & Johnson, M. (2008). *Metaphors we live by.* University of Chicago press.

Langdon, P., Clarkson, J., Robinson, P., Lazar, J., & Heylighen, A. (2012). *Designing Inclusive Systems.* Springer.

McLean, S. (2022). *Supporting children with neurodiversity.* Child Family Community Australia, Australian Institute of Family Studies.

Minow, M. (2021). EQUALITY VS. EQUITY. *American Journal of Law and Equality, 1*, 167–193. https://doi.org/10.1162/ajle_a_00019

Nicolaidis, C., Raymaker, D., Kapp, S. K., Baggs, A., Ashkenazy, E., McDonald, K., Weiner, M., Maslak, J., Hunter, M., & Joyce, A. (2019). The AASPIRE practice-based guidelines for the inclusion of autistic adults in research as co-researchers and study participants. *Autism, 23*(8), 2007–2019.

Nicolle, C., & Abascal, J. (2001). *Inclusive design guidelines for HCI.* CRC Press.

Null, R. (2013). *Universal design: Principles and models.* CRC Press.

Ostroff, E. (2011). Universal design: An evolving paradigm. *Universal Design Handbook.*

Persson, H., Åhman, H., Yngling, A. A., & Gulliksen, J. (2015). Universal design, inclusive design, accessible design, design for all: Different concepts—one goal? On the concept of accessibility—historical, methodological and philosophical aspects. *Universal Access in the Information Society, 14*, 505–526.

Ruiz, B., Pajares, J. L., Utray, F., & Moreno, L. (2011). Design for All in multimedia guides for museums. *Computers in Human Behavior, 27*(4), Article 4.

Shogren, K. A., Luckasson, R., & Schalock, R. L. (2021). Leveraging the power of context in disability policy development, implementation, and evaluation: Multiple applications to enhance personal outcomes. *Journal of Disability Policy Studies, 31*(4), 230–243.

Steinfeld, E., & Maisel, J. (2012). *Universal design: Creating inclusive environments.* John Wiley & Sons.

Stephanidis, C. (2021). Design for all in digital technologies. *Handbook of Human Factors and Ergonomics*, 1187–1215.

Sujan, J. S. R., Neumann, W. P., & Fels, D. I. (2017). *Human capability demands required from the elderly and disabled participants in the user centred design needs eliciatation methods—A survey study.*

Treviranus, J. (2010). One-Size-Fits-One Inclusive Learning. *PDF File. Cava Conference.*

Treviranus, J. (2024). Inclusive design: Valuing difference, recognizing complexity – introduction. In *Handbook of Disability* (pp. 755–778). Springer, Singapore. https://doi.org/10.1007/978-981-19-6056-7_98.

Waller, S., Bradley, M., Hosking, I., & Clarkson, P. J. (2015). Making the case for inclusive design. *Applied Ergonomics*, *46*, 297–303.

Web Content Accessibility Guidelines (WCAG) 2.1 (n.d.). Retrieved April 17, 2023, from https://www.w3.org/TR/WCAG21/

Zallio, M., & Clarkson, P. J. (2021). Inclusion, diversity, equity and accessibility in the built environment: A study of architectural design practice. *Building and Environment*, *206*, 108352.

2 Legislation, Regulations and Standards

Standards (technical and user interface), regulations, legislation, guidelines and best practices often guide accessibility and inclusion in organizations, institutions, governments and businesses. As a result, interaction with these entities as a researcher, contractor, business or consumer involves knowing the national, local, and international standards, regulations, legislation and best practices that apply in any specific context. However, knowing which standards and regulations to use can be overwhelming as there are potentially many possible options and jurisdictional considerations. In this chapter, examples from the broadcast industry and web accessibility in Canada are used to illustrate the different types of standards, regulations, legislation and guidelines that can apply to inclusivity.

Figure 2.1 shows a diagram of the different levels of legislation, regulations and standards with Canadian examples.

A brief overview of each of the items in Fig. 2.1 should provide the reader with a general perspective on how different items work together or can be used. For full legal interpretations of legislation, regulations or standards, the reader is referred to the actual published documents and legal precedents established with them. Some of the landmark cases for North America can be found in the reference section at the end of this chapter.

The use of legislation, regulations, standards, guidelines and best practices can be from multiple perspectives depending on how compliance is measured and/or rewarded, or how incompliance is tracked and penalized.

In Canada, the most generic and least detailed piece of legislation relating to the rights of all citizens is the Human Rights Act established in 1985 (Government of Canada 2021). In this Act, discriminatory practices are defined and the denial of access to a good, service, facility or accommodation is considered illegal. However, exceptions are allowed

D. Fels et al., *Inclusive Design Premises, Policies, Protocols, and Practices: From Usability to Empowerment*, Synthesis Lectures on Technology and Health,
https://doi.org/10.1007/978-3-032-15746-1_2

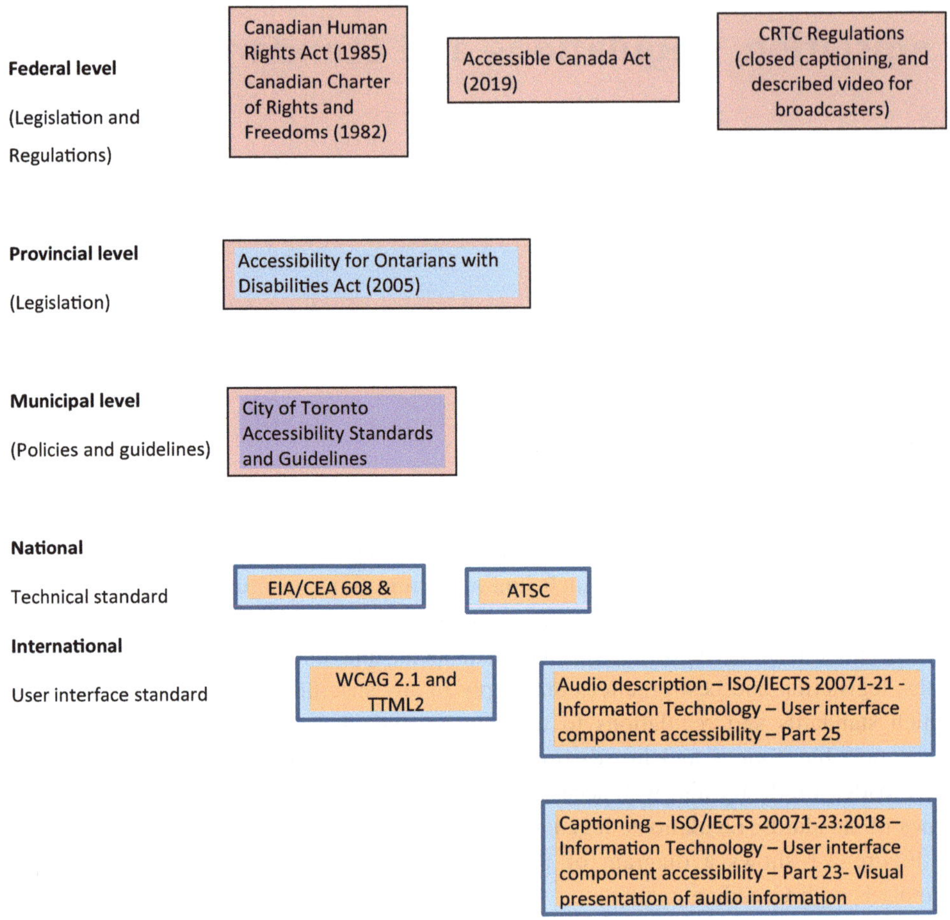

Fig. 2.1 Example of legislation and standards in Canada

as long as there is a demonstrated and *bona fide* justification. Often, an acceptable *bona fide* justification is financial hardship, which has been successfully used.

In 1995, H. Vlug brought a formal complaint against the Canadian Broadcasting Corporation (CBC) for discriminating against him by failing to provide closed captioning for all programming, which he claimed violated the Canadian Human Rights Act (Canadian Human Rights Reporter 2000). This case was brought to the Canadian Human Rights Tribunal, which hears complaints issued under this Act. In 2000, the Tribunal favoured Vlug's arguments from that of the broadcaster who claimed providing 100% captioning on all programs would present an undue financial to the company. The Tribunal was not satisfied that the CBC had sufficiently considered financial benefits and the real costs of providing closed captioning for all programs. The ruling in this case, however, only applied to a single broadcaster, the CBC, and no other. But, as a result of this landmark decision in Canada, in 2007, the Canadian Radio-television and Telecommunications Commission (CRTC) changed its regulations to require 100% captioning on all live and post-production English and French programs over the entire broadcast day (6 am to 11 pm) for most broadcasters in Canada (Government of Canada 2008). In 2009, this regulation was amended to include captioning requirements for advertising, sponsorship messages and promotional content (Government of Canada 2007).

Penalties for Canadian broadcasters who violate the CRTC captioning regulations can be issued upon broadcast license renewal that occurs every five years. License renewals are subjected to public hearings where complaints from the public can be submitted and considered. The types of penalties that can be imposed are: (1) warning to improve; (2) delay of license renewal; or (3) license cancellation.

As human rights legislation at the federal, state or provincial levels is often intentionally general and vague, it can be difficult, expensive and time-consuming to apply distinct accessibility or inclusion requirements to specific government groups, organizations or institutions. In addition, complaints must be brought against one organization rather than for an entire industry. As a result, governments often enact more specific legislation and/or policies that relate to inclusive and accessible practices. These provide more pragmatic and specific directives to public and private-sector organizations and institutions. In some instances, these directives become regulations to which legislation can refer.

An example in the Canadian context is the Canadian Radio-television and Telecommunications Commission (CRTC), which regulates and licenses access to the electromagnetic spectrum in Canada (e.g., broadcast television or radio channels), and is the agency enabled by the Broadcasting Act in Canada. Included in the broadcast regulations, and mandated for most broadcasters, are specifications for quantity and quality of access to broadcast media for people who are Deaf/Hard of Hearing, Blind or Low Vision. However, these regulations only apply to broadcast materials and content that are controlled by the broadcast companies (e.g., broadcast over-the-air, on cable or satellite services, or streamed), and do not include access to other Internet-based media such as posts on social media.

Other sources of inclusive practices are national or international standards established by interested representatives (individuals, consumers, industries, academics, and "experts") but often not governments. These are meant to be applied widely and without specific references to government legislation, regulations, or mandates. However, they are often used and referred to by government legislation as a way of measuring compliance with legislation or polices related to accessibility and inclusion. An example of an international standard is the Web Content Accessibility Guidelines 2.1 established and maintain by the World Wide Web Consortium (*Web Content Accessibility Guidelines (WCAG) 2.1*, n.d.-a). These standards are used and accepted by many countries and regions throughout the world. An example of a regional standard is the Ofcom's Code on Television Access Services that regulates captioning (subtitling for the hard of hearing) only in the UK

(Ofcom 2021). Most countries and regions use both types of standards in their inclusion laws and policies.

These standards are usually sanctioned and published by international or national standards bodies, such as the International Standards Organization (ISO), the World Wide Web Consortium (W3C), Consumer Electronics Association (in the US), Institute of Electronic and Electrical Engineers (in the US), Canadian Standards Association (in Canada), etc. that have been established to create and monitor standards. Detailed rules, criteria and best practices about "what" and "how" to do it in order to achieve good/optimal accessibility practices are established by agreement, or majority vote from the group of representatives participating in generating, describing, and sanctioning these practices. The dichotomy of standards falls into technical and user interface standards. Technical standards outline specific formats, electrical specifications, and technical details for signal processing and file formats that would affect hardware and low-level software processing whereas, user interaction standards relate to what is provided to the user through the user interface. Technical standards outline how a particular element is realized and should be processed by equipment, while user interaction standards outline what a user can expect to see/hear/manipulate.

An example of a user interface standard is the Web Content Accessibility Guidelines (WCAG) 2.1. This document applies to web accessibility standards that apply at three different levels, A, AA and AAA where the A level is a most basic accessibility requirement and AAA provides the greatest accessibility to the most people. For example, captioning guidelines relate to time-based media. To achieve a Level A for Guideline 1.2-Time-based Media, "Captions are provided for all prerecorded audio content in synchronized media, except when the media is a media alternative for text and is clearly labelled as such" (*Web Content Accessibility Guidelines (WCAG) 2.1*, n.d. Para 52). In order to meet a higher standard, Level AA for Captions (Live) states, "Captions are provided for all live audio content in synchronized media" (*Web Content Accessibility Guidelines (WCAG) 2.1* n.d. para 54), and finally the highest level, Level AAA, for Time-based Media for Audio-only material would be "An alternative for time-based media that presents equivalent information for live audio-only content is provided" (*Web Content Accessibility Guidelines (WCAG) 2.1* n.d., para 59).

Examples of how the WCAG 2.1 standard is used in different government legislation appear in the Web Accessibility requirements in Canada's federal Accessible Canada Act, Ontario's Accessibility for Ontarians with Disabilities Act and the City of Toronto's Standards and Guidelines for Accessibility, which all refer to WCAG 2.1 Level AA as the requirements for compliance with that particular legislation or policy in those jurisdictions.

An example of a technical standard that relates to captioning is CTA-708 (Advanced Television Systems Committee 2017) which details how a caption should be packaged and delivered for a digital television broadcast in North America. For example, CEA-708 specifies which fonts and colours are acceptable, the maximum characters per line, what

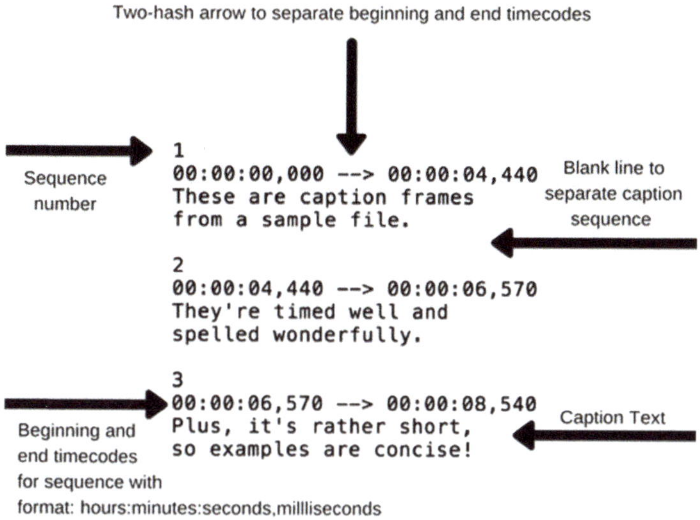

Fig. 2.2 .srt file specification (Mahoney 2021, para 4)

data are required in a caption file, and how a caption file/signal should be processed by televised broadcast. A file format standard, such as the basic.srt file format, specifies what information is required in a caption file, and the order and style of that information (see Fig. 2.2). Compare this file format with a more modern caption file format for the World Wide Web, the WebVTT format (see Fig. 2.3).

Technical standards allow hardware manufactures and software developers to create equipment and software that will accept and effectively process the information presented in these standard formats. Users then can be confident that when they purchase equipment or software, the data, information and signals will be properly processed and made available without having to understand or be concerned about any low-level processing or setup; "they press a button and it works" regardless of the hardware, signal or software source.

The world of laws, regulations, standards, guidelines and best practices that relate to inclusion can be overwhelming and difficult to navigate as they are often written in legal and/or convoluted language. Inclusive designers, developers, consultants, and researchers must be aware of the various levels, and know which ones apply to a specific situation. Becoming involved in the production of standards and guidelines can be one way of staying up-to-date as well as bringing specific expertise, experience and evidence to the table, which, in turn, will affect those standards, guidelines, best practices and regulations. Disability advocacy organizations also often participate in the development of standards and guidelines, which may provide another avenue to engage with those standards and guidelines.

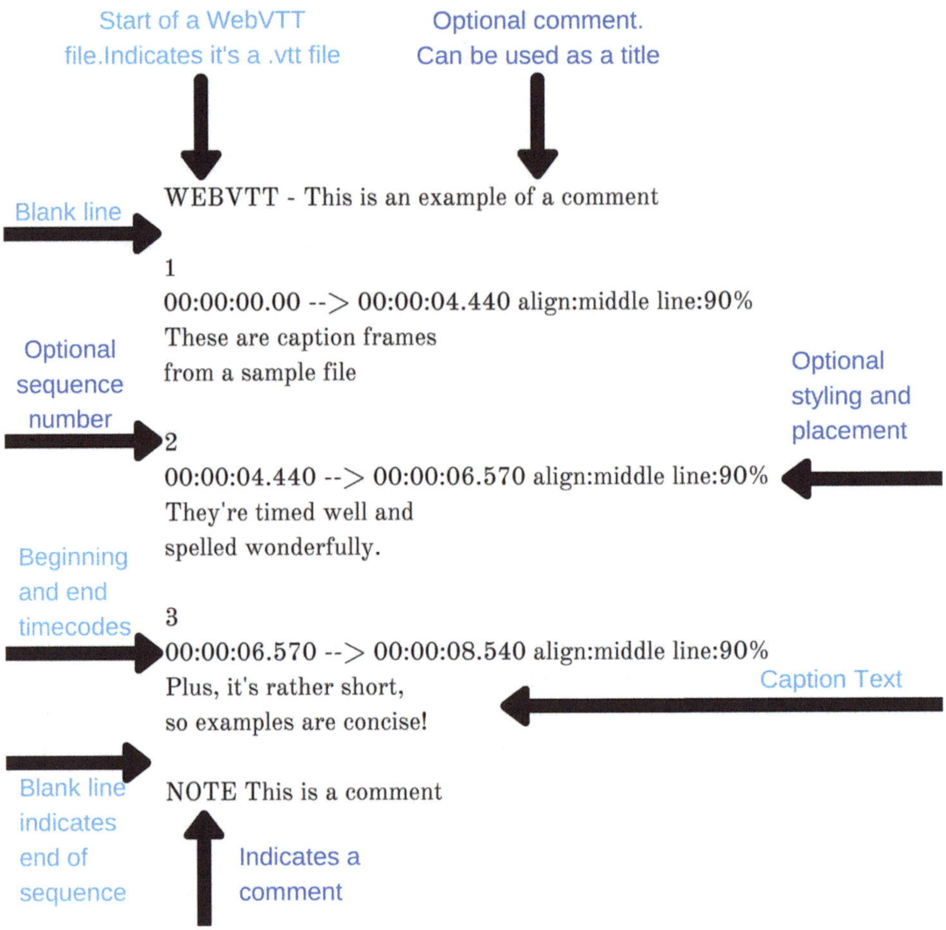

Fig. 2.3 WebVTT file format. Note that there is allowance for alignment, and styling elements (Klein 2021)

2.1 Exercises and Questions for Reflection

1. Choose an inclusion topic that you would like to find legislation, regulations, standards and best practices on for your region.
2. Create a table similar to Fig. 2.1 for your own country, state, and city for this topic. Which laws apply? Which standards apply? Which best practices apply? What laws, regulations, policies and standards would you use and why?
3. If you wanted to sue someone about lack of captioning in their materials, which legislation, and/or regulations would apply and why for one of the following options?
   - A cable channel in your country

  - A school board in the city
  - A grocery store chain in your region
  - A government website with video training materials
4. In your region, which agencies, individuals or organization could you ask for assistance to find out whether you have a case or not?
5. What legal cases about inclusion have occurred in your city, region or country? What were these cases about, which laws, regulations or standards were used, and what was the result(s)?

References

Advanced Television Systems Committee. (2017). ATSC Standard: Captions and Subtitles (A/343) (A/343: 2017). https://www.atsc.org/wp-content/uploads/2016/12/A343-2017-Captions-and-Subtitles-4.pdf

Canadian Human Rights Reporter. (2000). Human Rights Digest. 8. https://www.canlii.org/en/commentary/doc/2000CanLIIDocs336#!fragment/zoupio-_Tocpdf_bk_11/BQCwhgziBcwMYgK4DsDWszIQewE4BUBTADwBdoAvbRABwEtsBaAfX2zhoBMAzZgI1TMAjEICUAGmTZShCAEVEhXAE9oAcjXiIhMLgQKlqjVp16QAZTykAQqoBKAUQAyDgGoBBAHIBhB+NJgfNCk7KKiQA

Government of Canada, L. S. (2021, August 31). Consolidated federal laws of Canada, Canadian Human Rights Act. Justice Laws Website. https://laws-lois.justice.gc.ca/eng/acts/H-6/page-1.html

Government of Canada, C. R. and T. C. (CRTC). (2007, May 17). ARCHIVED - Broadcasting Public Notice CRTC 2007-54 [Regulatory policies]. https://crtc.gc.ca/eng/archive/2007/pb2007-54.htm

Government of Canada, C. R. and T. C. (CRTC). (2008, December 11). TV Access for People who are Deaf or Hard of Hearing: Closed Captioning [Consumer information]. https://crtc.gc.ca/eng/info_sht/b321.htm

Government of Canada, D. of J. (2021, March 15). The Canadian Charter of Rights and Freedoms. https://www.justice.gc.ca/eng/csj-sjc/rfc-dlc/ccrf-ccdl/

Klein, R. (2021, June 9). WebVTT Captions: How to Create a Web Video Text Track File. 3Play Media. https://www.3playmedia.com/blog/how-to-create-a-webvtt-file/

Mahoney, K. (2021, May 25). Your Complete Guide on How to Create an SRT File. 3Play Media. https://www.3playmedia.com/blog/create-srt-file/

Ofcom. (2021). Ofcom's code on television access services (pp. 1–20). https://www.ofcom.org.uk/tv-radio-and-on-demand/broadcast-codes/tv-access-services

Web Content Accessibility Guidelines (WCAG) 2.1. (n.d.). Retrieved April 17, 2023, from https://www.w3.org/TR/WCAG21/

Landmark Cases in Broadcasting and Theatre

Audio description for Hamilton (https://www.courtlistener.com/docket/4573489/1/lasser-v-nederlander-organization-inc/)

National Association of the Deaf vs Netflix Inc.
Netflix (https://www.3playmedia.com/2017/04/05/audio-description-lawsuits/)
Vlug vs CBC (Canadian Human Rights Reporter, 2000)

Transportation

Lepofsky v. Toronto Transit Commission (2005). http://www.ohrc.on.ca/en/next-stop-accessibility-report-public-transit-stop-announcements-ontario/background-accessible-transit-and-stop-announcements.

Web Accessibility

2010. Jodhan vs Canada. https://ca.vlex.com/vid/jodhan-v-can-g-680663097

Inclusive Teaching for Instructors and Teaching Assistants

3

The purpose of this chapter is to provide a framework for instructors and graduate students to approach inclusive teaching that focuses on students with disabilities (SWD). This chapter is not a how to do manual; rather, it is about enhancing and developing critical thinking skills for effective inclusive teaching focusing on SWD inclusion. At the end of the chapter there are three reflections on the experience of being an inclusive instructor, one from each of three authors of this book. These reflections offer a unique perspective on different approaches taken, which challenge some of the current guidelines.

3.1 Introduction

One of the duties of academics is teaching or supporting the teaching of undergraduate and graduate students. In the spirit of meeting equity, diversity, and inclusivity mandates or goals including the one by United Nations 2030 Sustainable Development Goals (United Nations 2023), educational institutions have created supports and programs for SWD e.g., accommodations such as use of screen readers and extra time for assignments and tests. Additionally, the provision of accommodation services is governed by the local laws in the country where the instruction is taking place. For instance, in Canada, it is governed by the Accessible Canada Act (Branch 2019; Canada 2020), Canadian Charter of Rights and Freedoms, (D. of J. Government of Canada 2021) and provincial accessibility regulations including, the Accessibility for Ontarians With Disabilities Act in Ontario (Ontario 2005). US federal laws that govern educational accommodations are Section 504 of the

D. Fels et al., *Inclusive Design Premises, Policies, Protocols, and Practices: From Usability to Empowerment*, Synthesis Lectures on Technology and Health,
https://doi.org/10.1007/978-3-032-15746-1_3

Rehabilitation Act of 1973 (Office of the assistant secretary for administration and management n.d.), Americans with Disabilities Act (ADA 1991), Individuals with Disabilities Education Act (*Individuals with Disabilities Education Act (IDEA)* n.d.).

While there is a range of academic accommodations, a common type of accommodation is provision of additional time for assignments, tests, quizzes and exams. Instructors, and teaching and graduate assistants, are usually notified about specific accommodations for students and are expected to implement them in their classes; it is assumed that instructors and teaching assistants (TAs) know how to do this. There are usually guidelines and training opportunities offered through academic institutions or services for learning about different accommodations and how to integrate them into courses as well as other private and not-for-profit sector offerings of training, workshops and educational materials and resources on how to teach accessibility to designers/developers in various disciplines and courses such as Computer Science and Game Design (see https://teachaccess.org/teach-access-by-design/ for an example of offerings from the non-profit sector and graduate program in Inclusive Design at OCAD University https://gradadmissions.ocadu.ca/program/INCD as an example of a full program at an academic institution). However, inclusive teaching goes beyond accommodations endorsed by the institution: It is a way of thinking and being. Having an inclusive sensibility means having space to listen to students, being flexible and fully present in attending to barriers that occur in classes that limit participation [for a Canadian legal definition of barrier please refer to the Accessible Canada Act (Canada 2020)]. In this chapter, a brief overview on different types of accommodations is presented followed by an outline of how to foster an embedded and creative approach to inclusive teaching that asks the reader to question the utility and applicability of standardized practices and procedures, such as assessments (e.g., Nieminen 2022) to foster fairness and inclusion in all aspects of teaching.

3.2 Learning Environments

Post-secondary education is constantly evolving in learning environments, some of which are a result of innovative hardware and software technologies. These technologies are usually designed for able-bodied users, and continue to serve able-bodied students, which can create some learning barriers for SWD. These barriers can prevent SWD from entering or successfully completing their learning goals.

Many post-secondary institutions have centralized disability or accommodation services, including disability resource centres (Li et al. 2023). SWD will receive coordinated supports upon medical documentation of a disability, e.g. MIT requires assessment to be done by medical professionals (Massachusetts Institute of Technology n.d.), the level of quality and quantity of services varies across institutions through those services. They are also generally underfunded compared to the number of students served (Dolmage 2017), and saddled with institutional practices, conventions and administrative processes that are not always aligned with student's schedules, generating delays and preventing needed action to occur on a timely basis for SWD. In addition, many SWD choose not to disclose their disability or have not been officially diagnosed (Dolmage 2017). As a result, SWD can be at a disadvantage from the start given the time-intensive process required to generate the documents necessary to qualify for an accommodation, further delaying the accommodation itself.

Learning environments are dynamic, ranging from in-person or online (using video conferencing platforms such as Google Meets™), slide delivery, audio-video presentations in lecture halls, to hands-on group or individual activities in computer and material laboratories. Teaching methods and assessments come in a wide variety, e.g., individual assignments, tests, exams, group work and presentations.

Accommodations provided to SWD are individualized tools that support access, and they vary from student to student and across majors and experiences (Newman et al. 2021). There is no 'one-size-fits-all'. In order to ensure that SWD are included, which requires moving beyond the one-size-fits-all paradigm, flexibility and creativity are needed to implement inclusive practices and embody inclusive teaching. First attempts may incur mistakes, but one should not be discouraged or abandon attempting to institute inclusive teaching practices. Instructors and TAs need to accept a shared responsibility with accommodation services and the institution. This can be a tall order for many instructors and TAs who may have limited training, interest, understanding of inclusive teaching practices, or who may have tried to initiate a solution unsuccessfully in the past, or who are concerned about their notion of 'fairness', or be suspicious of SWD.

To prepare for carrying out inclusive teaching centring on SWD, an understanding of how the learning environments are affecting them in order to be able to address the root of barriers facing students. Instead of considering disability as a constraint to individual success, and requiring an expert to determine some sort of accommodation, successful instructors of SWD are able to be flexible in order to examine their teaching practices through an inclusive lens.

3.3 Accommodation Processes

Established institutional procedures surrounding accommodation have been constructed from an ableist framework, and continue to prioritize this perspective (Kaundinya and Schroth 2022). The process begins prior to SWD entering classrooms, tutorial or lab environments, and participating in requisite medical processes in order to substantiate and validate their legal right to access barrier-free education/instruction.

Instead, often the beginning of the process begins when an SWD completes a request for accommodations at the academic institution and then working through the approval process before any communication is sent to instructors. The approval process usually requires medical documentation. This involves a doctor's note and a series of standardized tests, such as a psychoeducational assessment completed by specialists, with measurable data for interpretation by certain professionals (e.g., an audiogram documenting hearing loss to be interpreted by audiologist), to provide evidence and justification for the SWD's differential learning needs. The process of accessing medical professionals to complete these tests can be cost/time prohibitive for SWD and their families, lengthening or rendering academic accommodation obsolete (Bickenbach et al. 2016). Families of and SWD's may also be unaware of the existence of accommodation services (Lyman et al. 2016). This process results in SWD being responsible for accommodation instead of the institution and instructors.

Furthermore, by placing accessibility into the control of healthcare providers; racialized, indigenous, and non-gender conforming SWD can be further stigmatized in accessing their learning needs/rights equitably, given historical discrimination and abuse, and continued lack of trust from these communities (Lezzoni et al. 2021).

They also suggest that healthcare providers typically are not educators, or lack direct experience or training in effective inclusive teaching methods. Although healthcare providers are responsible for assessing and recommending accommodations for SWD, their approach tends to be superficial and categorical. Their knowledge and understanding of how accommodations function and are used by SWD, instructors and academic institutions may be approximate and outdated.

The tasks required of students to successfully receive accommodations and the reliance on medical assessments turns inclusion into medically-mediated and lengthy processes, whereby SWD are often perceived as a homogeneous group (Taneja-Johansson 2021) in the accommodation process rather than included and valued for their lived experiences and expertise in addressing barriers in the learning environments (virtual and in-person), and within teaching and assessment practices. Accommodations that are prescribed will rarely address (or even be considered useful to SWD themselves) the necessary, ongoing and often new or unexpected ways in which one might support a SWD in order to enable equivalent curriculum content access (Toutain 2019). For example, the concept of "extra time", a common accessibility accommodation in post-secondary education, can have implications beyond extending formal testing in a specialized space, and requires more holistic and creative thinking. "Extra time" will be addressed in Sect. 3.4.1.

3.4 Inclusive Teaching and Learning

Teaching and learning is not limited to traditional methods, such as lectures, paper-based exams, and text-based assignments. It also does not take place only during traditional business hours (e.g., Monday to Friday, 9 am to 5 pm). As a result of the COVID pandemic and technological advances, many new approaches to teaching and learning have expanded the possible alternatives to traditional methods. Several examples of new methods include students using multimedia technology to produce video assignments or responses to tests; having text-based real-time captioning available for live video conferencing sessions and follow-up transcripts; and asynchronously delivering content followed by discussion and reflection exercises.

The concept of fairness, in relation to standardization in teaching and evaluation instruments, is often a stated goal of instructors and TAs (Kane 2020). As applied in the context of SWD, it can become more complex and difficult to achieve, as there are many ways in which something can be 'unfair'. Also, there are differing frames of reference that could be used. For example, does fairness compare between disabled and non-disabled students, or just in the context of one particular student's constraints and needs? Fairness is also one way to look at inclusion and equity, where equity means that every individual has what they need to succeed. SWD who have been treated fairly and have equity, are able to succeed in the learning environment (Rasooli et al. 2021). Fairness supports treating SWD from an individual perspective, valuing them and their strengths rather than trying to compare them with others. It then becomes incumbent on instructors and TAs to think creatively and from an equity and fairness perspective, rather than simply limiting any actions to exactly what the letter from the accommodation service says. Section 3.4.1, provides a discussion of time from a fairness and equity perspective with respect to possible constraints and needs.

3.4.1 Considering Time Accommodation as Equity and Inclusion

This section provides a detailed examination of time accommodation as an inclusive practice. Its purpose is to present a framework that instructors can use when they receive a letter for time accommodation, or there is a request by a student for more time. Time accommodation is one of the most common in the form of extra time for formal evaluations (e.g., exams, quizzes, mid-terms, etc.), or for assignments (Edwards et al. 2022). This extra time accommodation assumes that there is a 'standard' time and format allocated to the test by the instructor and there is no flexibility in the test design; it is necessary to have the 'same' test for all.

From an equity and inclusion perspective, these assumptions should be challenged. For example, requiring an individual to attend to one task for extended lengths of time can be physically and cognitively fatiguing due to increased physical and mental stress, which can reduce the individual's ability to perform that task efficiently and effectively, even with breaks (Smith et al. 2019). SWD who are provided with extra time to complete a test are working longer than other students. Although there is some evidence that extra time does not necessarily have an impact on fatigue or performance on specific types of tests [e.g., Laitusis et al. (2007) examined results from the Scholastic Aptitude Test (SAT) multiple-choice reasoning test; (Lovett and Nelson 2021), other factors such as test type, ability to concentrate, and disability factors may influence test performance (Hurwitz et al.

2007)]. More research on how test type affects fatigue or test performance is needed in order to substantiate claims made in research.

The influence of the many possible factors that affect a student's performance over time and need for accommodations requires considerably more study. However, from general Human Factors literature, sustained work results in increased cognitive and physical workload (Lean and Shan 2012). For example, if a student is given 4-h to complete a test that is designed to be completed in 2-h, that student must be 'sitting' at a testing centre for 4-h. That student experiences mental and physical stress for a sustained period; double the amount of time that others writing the 2-h test must endure. This does not account for the extra time that SWD often need for transportation, access to resources, and advocating for their needs, which only adds to the time differences between different types of students.

Therefore, if taken as a whole, the incremental time it takes a SWD to achieve the same tasks as an able-bodied student (such as getting ready, commuting to school, explaining accommodation needs, securing notes, taking tests, and returning home) can have an increased negative psychological and physical toll, especially for those who are already marginalized. This is considered neither an equitable nor inclusive practice.

In order to be inclusive and equitable, an instructor needs to think more broadly about the notion and implications of extra-time accommodations. Table 3.1 shows a framework for considering the cognitive, physical tasks, potential equity issues required of test taking students, using example of a time-based multiple-choice style of test. As part of the framework, test modifications are suggested here to demonstrate how the tasks and issues are addressed to provide inclusion and equity to SWD students.

3.4.2 Group Work

One of the least considered constraints for accommodations is group work. The purpose of group work is typically to allow peer-to-peer learning (Boud et al. 1999). However, group interactions and dynamics could cause conflict or not be accessible, thus reducing opportunities for peer learning. Conflict in groups can result from different issues, but common ones include, a member's perception of another member 'not doing their share of work', missing internal deadlines, and grade distribution. Accommodations do not often extend to group work even though it may be necessary. Group members may not have the interpersonal or communication skills to interact with each other. They may need training or specialized knowledge to work together. For example, students may not know how to adjust their speaking pace and/or work with the interpreter so that they are understood by Deaf/HOH student(s). Students may be overwhelmed with speaking in front of other students, or fast-paced, overlapping talk may exclude some students. These difficulties may result in exclusionary practices within the group, which may, in turn,

Table 3.1 Equity and inclusion framework design and implementation with an example for hand-written closed-book multiple choice test

Test purpose and technique	Cognitive demands	Physical/perceptual demands	Potential equity issues	Test modifications for inclusion
Evaluate knowledge and understanding of course content by answering 100 multiple choice questions based on course materials in a 2-h closed-book test	• *Reading, memorizing* written, and audio-visual course materials prior to test • *Recognizing* memorized items, terms, and information • *Reading* written questions and possible answers on the test • *Differentiating* right and wrong items in a set of options • *Time management* • *Prioritize and structure* answering process (e.g., order of answering questions, uncertainty, reviewing)	• Physically *marking* responses on bubbles on a paper form with pencil held in a hand • *Sitting* at a desk for 2-h with no break • Seeing and visually processing words on paper	• Visual tasks (reading) may take longer times (for SWD with reading, print, learning or information processing disabilities) • Sitting and focusing on a multiple-choice exam for more than 2-h can be fatiguing; the longer the time, the more fatiguing it is • Listening to questions and answers being read (e.g., by a screen reader) requires extra audio processing and attention • Watching an interpreter sign questions and answers requires more visual attention than reading (visual information in sign language is complex and requires more continuous and sustained focus)	Use time as the common element instead of 'the test' • Complete 50 questions in 2-h instead of 100 in 4-h OR/AND • Offer an oral exam of equivalent questions for students using sign language or screen readers. Time limited to 2-h

affect a willingness to interact and complete tasks. It may also affect group formations, where some individuals are excluded as result of lack of accommodations in group work.

There are various ways to reduce conflict and support interaction in groups. But each situation is unique and requires flexibility and creativity as not every group has the same dynamic. One way to approach this is to consider what would benefit everyone regardless of their abilities. For example, reducing the number of students in a group (e.g., pairs), having students learn how to take turns so that all members are included (e.g., using a 'talking' stick, Fujioka 1998), and enacting a mutual agreement on working pace. Instructor can model speaking pace in order for students to observe how to be inclusive. Also, design group work so students do not feel pressured to work faster to accomplish work (e.g., given only 5-min to read the 2-page hand out, then discuss and develop an answer may be insufficient time for SWD; more time may be needed).

3.4.3 Help and Assistance

Using the words 'help' or 'assistance' can be loaded and subjective terms for SWD (Kulkarni 2012). In some situations, there is no request for help by SWD, but help is still provided without asking and done *to* the person, rather than with them. Unrequested help can be triggering for some SWD or create more barriers when the help is not needed or wrong kind of support is provided. Holding a person's arm to 'help' with navigating space, moving a mobility device, or interpreting for someone without consent, or a request when not trained are examples of well-intentioned actions that may be harmful to, or impede learning. To avoid harmful 'help' or violating consent, a discussion/instruction on what help/assistance means for course work and group work, and for individuals is necessary. Guidance on this topic can be found in formalized guidelines (e.g., Stevens 2003; Toolkit 2020) as well as by asking the individuals involved to discuss what, how they perceive and want 'help'.

3.5 Being an Inclusive Instructor or Teaching Assistant

There are numerous guidelines and 'how-to' resources to learn about inclusive teaching practices (e.g., Dewsbury and Brame 2019; Finkelstein et al. 2021; Sanger 2020; Sathy and Hogan 2019; *Teach Access by Design—Teach Access* n.d.). As an introduction to striving towards becoming an inclusive instructor or TA, we have outlined seven topics to begin this process.

1. Having an Inclusive Mindset Goal: Create learning environments that value and respect SWD and their diverse backgrounds. Instructors appreciate unique experiences and perspectives that each student can bring to the classroom. The inclusive mindset can

help create a welcoming learning environment. It can help foster a sense of belonging in SWD and support the notion that SWD need equal opportunities to succeed. This respect and appreciation by instructors can be conveyed in different tangible and measurable ways. For example:

(a) Develop an inclusive syllabus with elements such as:
  (i) Describing how the instructor will actively work to support all students including SWD by modifying teaching materials.
  (ii) Providing a list or description of resources to all students, e.g., CART, speech-to-text tools for students to use, links to disabled student groups/networks.
  (iii) Providing options for communication with instructor, e.g., email, voice/video message, zoom or in person.
  (iv) Using clear rubrics with examples of what meets each criterion A, B, etc.

(b) When interacting with SWD: Do not ask personal questions about their disability(ies), body function, or mental function.

(c) Design inclusion into the course from the beginning (see University of Minnesota 2023, for an example of how to do this).

(d) SWD are learning how to self-advocate and may need assistance and patience with that. Often parents, social workers, teachers, and other interested parties from elementary and high school days were the student's advocate, and self-advocacy skills were not taught or developed. Be patient and offer suggestions for tools and resources.

(e) Encourage all students to learn how to describe their learning needs to normalize self-advocacy in educational situations and reduce stigma around SWD.

2. Limitations in Accommodations:

(a) ASL-English interpreters may not know the jargon or technical terms in the course in either academic ASL or English. Academic interpreting is highly specialized and requires advanced training with years of study and practice in two languages. When interpreters do not have the experience and training, there are more errors made in the interpreted content (Gany et al. 2007). Errors can result in different meaning being provided, information left out, or/and confusing messages being delivered. As result SWD are not necessarily being taught the same material as non-SWD.

(b) Technical issues in teaching and learning environment
  (i) Classrooms can have low lighting conditions particularly when data projectors are used. The interpreter in the room cannot be seen by the Deaf student.
  (ii) The sign language interpreter cannot be seen clearly by the Deaf student e.g., the interpreter is standing in front of the window with the sunlight shining through making it difficult to see their face/hands. Computer equipment is blocking the view of interpreter. In a virtual setting, the interpreter is not shown as a participant in the video conferencing platform.

(iii) There is no microphone/audio available for presenters (students or instructors). As a result, individuals must rely on their own ability to project a sufficiently loud speaking voice. This can also be affected by room size, noise levels, and echo.
(iv) Live captioning is not turned on in the video-conferencing based platform.
(v) Speech-to-text accommodations are not checked for errors (spelling or gaps due to internet issues).
(vi) An in-classroom captioner (called CART service), may not hear what was said resulting in missed content.
(vii) Some online platforms are designed to follow sound of a person speaking which is a barrier for Deaf students who use ASL to get attention.

(c) Preparation notes are delivered late or not delivered at all to the sign language interpreter, notetaker, or student. Errors in interpreting can be aggravated when interpreters do not have sufficient preparation or review time for what will be taught. Interpreters may not have interpreted for a particular course and need to review the materials to familiarize themselves with the content and jargon. Remember, sign language interpreters are neither students nor experts in the academic fields being taught in class. Also, ASL is not a translation of English but rather its own language with different grammar, and conceptual expressions similar to any other language.

3. Meet with students to understand their needs and ask what works best for them in the course:
   (a) Offer to be available beyond office hours using different formats/tools (e.g., video conferencing, email, etc.).
4. Provide opportunities for ongoing student feedback/check-ins. Ask questions such as:
   (a) Does the student have access to the materials/technology/system and is it working for them?
   (b) Is the accommodation being provided working?
5. Be flexible and prepare ahead of time.
   (a) Consider technological and media alternatives.
6. Ask for help from others when things are unclear or uncertain. It is ok to make mistakes.
7. Learn about being inclusive and accepting of alternative practices from examples.
   (a) SWD who are neurodiverse. There is increase in number of neurodiverse students in higher education. Understanding their challenges and experiences including the stigma they experience and acknowledging that stigma is needed (Clouder et al. 2020).
      (i) Provide examples in course content showing neurodiverse individuals or their work.
      (ii) Design course content delivery to chunk content.

(iii) Use bullet points, and graphics to reinforce message. Note: for students who are Blind/Low Vision, the graphics will need to be explained.
(iv) Content delivery is consistent with detailed instructions.
(v) Model how the work is to be done, provide examples of work and/or templates.
(vi) Flexibility and creativity may be needed for supporting alternative methods of in-class communication e.g., an anonymous poll for the whole class,
   1. How would this type of student prefer to communicate with the students in a group?
   2. How would this type of student prefer to communicate in the class?
   3. What are text and voice (recorded/face-to-face) alternatives?

3.6 First Person Perspectives from the Author's Lived Experiences

In this section, the three authors who compiled this chapter and who have extensive experience in teaching SWD share their first-hand insights and experiences with one example each. Drawing upon their diverse backgrounds, including one Deaf author who has personally navigated the educational system as a SWD and later became a successful instructor of SWD, they offer valuable insights and their own strategies on how to make meaningful changes to teaching practices that foster inclusivity. The examples shared here are not representative of all SWD. The purpose is to provide a model for educators and practitioners who aim to improve their inclusive approaches and ensure academic success for all students.

3.6.1 An Example for Online Instruction with a Student with ADHD and Undiagnosed Mobility Disability

I noticed that a student was falling behind in completing assignments, despite being active in online Zoom™ sessions. I sent an email to the student reminding them of my office hours and inquiring about their assignments. I wrote, "*I noticed that your assignments have not been turned in yet. Is everything ok?*" During my office hours, the student confided in me that they were having difficulty completing assignments. They had recently been diagnosed with ADHD, and also were experiencing anxiety about their new diagnose and were facing mobility issues with their hands.

I followed up by asking them what they needed. The initial response was that, they didn't know. I continued with patience, allowing them time to reflect and respond. I modelled the behaviour I wanted to convey while describing it to reassure the student. I took a couple of deep breaths while suggesting, *let's take the time to focus and collect our thoughts*. I offered the student the option to take a break or resume the activity. The student wanted to resume.

I rephrased my question and narrowed my focus to one specific assignment type that I noticed they were struggling with the most. I made sure to regulate my breathing, keeping it even and, calm, as I communicated with the student. I checked my facial expression to ensure it was friendly and relaxed, and I maintained an open and relaxed posture. I expressed my willingness to learn and improve and offered my support finding effective solutions for success. I sat back and waited. I remained present, focused, and refrained from checking the time. Some SWD students may shut down if they perceive that the other person is not fully attentive to them. This approach of slowing down, stating the purpose of my questions, and ensuring that my body language matched my intent was effective with this student. The student then shared with me that they had difficulty discerning the specific requirements from the assignment description. They needed highly detailed step-by-step instructions. This feedback also helped me to realize my mistakes which were that some instructions I provided were vague. After receiving feedback from the student, I revised the assignment descriptions to include more detailed instructions. To make the assignment more manageable, I broke it down into smaller sections, thereby spreading the workload across the week. Due dates for each section were assigned to help the student stay on track and avoid feeling overwhelmed with one large weekly deadline. Some SWD may struggle with organizing their weekly workload and require specific instructions to effectively manage their tasks.

I created an overview page for the week to be posted in Canvas which was the platform used to manage the online course instruction. Here is an example.

1. Read Chapter X, pages Y to Z in book ABC by Tuesday, (insert date).
2. Read the questions (please see the link for provided) by Tuesday.
3. Reread the chapter and review the rubric for answering the questions, develop your answers by writing or sketching out your ideas on scrap paper to practice answering by Wednesday.
4. Post your answers in the discussion post by Thursday.
5. Read two of your classmates' discussion posts by Friday.
6. Read the rubric for responding to classmates' posts by Friday.
7. Review the rubric for what is required to respond to your classmate's post and, develop your answers by writing or sketching your ideas on scrap paper by Monday.
8. To finish participating in the online discussion, respond to your classmates by Monday (insert date).

I made some suggestions regarding time management such as take breaks for about 15 min every hour or so (Costales et al. 2021). I explained the Pomodoro Technique and how I have applied to in my studies and current job. I gently pointed out that each individual's body responds differently to time cues, and there are various options available such as, visual cues, vibration, and audio alerts in the form of timers. The student was not aware of either the Pomodoro Technique or the various options for setting cues with a timer or alarm.

I inquired if they were aware of any speech-to-text tools that could assist them with their mobility difficulties. They were unaware of these tools. I provided links to two distinct speech-to-text applications such as Otter AI™. I demonstrated how those tools work and their limitations.

I also informed the student they could submit an "oral assignment" instead of a written one. Other options were to record their assignments on video or present their papers in-person during office hours, which would reduce the physical effort of using their hands for typing.

During my session with the student, I identified additional areas of difficulty, including understanding rubrics and their application, as well as participating effectively in online discussions with classmates. I have modified my course by adding additional content that includes links to various resources for students. Here are some of the examples of the modifications:

- A description of the purpose of a rubric (Cornell University provides guidance on how students can utilize a rubric as a self-assessment guide).
- Free speech-to-text tools available in Google Doc, Otter AI, and in the Zoom app.
- The Pomodoro Technique
- Recorded lectures and presentations the explain the alternative formats for exams and assignments.
- A recorded video has been included to provide additional instructions on assignments and the step-by-step methods of breaking down assignments into smaller components.

I also announced the availability of these tools, using student-friendly language on the learning management system in order to encourage their use and make them more widely known. All students were able to achieve their learning goals in my course and apply the tools and methods they learned to other courses. The student with ADHD used the speech-to text-tools for their assignments, and was were able to achieve high grades in the course due to the implementation of inclusive methods.

I viewed my work with the SWD as an opportunity to grow as a teacher. I also made modifications to my other courses wherever possible. This will benefit future students, SWD and other students, in a similar way to how "curb cuts" benefit users of mobility devices and others. Rao and Tanners (2011) describe how design of a course for SWD is a curb cut benefiting all students.

I had follow-up conversations with on-campus tech support services for students and shared my experience with others via email which took very little time. I shared my knowledge on effective inclusive teaching and requested additional resources on campus for SWD including the resources I have developed. I contributed to the university service by leading a workshop on how to write an inclusive syllabus for instructors. That was how I advocated for SWD.

3.6.2 Being a Student Ombudsperson as a Professor

I took on the role of ombudsperson for SWD in my department after noticing that SWD faced difficulties advocating for themselves, particularly with instructors who were either incapable or unwilling to consider accessibility needs to accommodate them. Furthermore, some instructors expressed concerns about accommodations being unjust to students without disabilities or viewed them as a means of 'cheating' (an attitudinal barrier). For instance, one instructor mistakenly believed that sign language interpreters were '*telling the student what the answers on the test were supposed to be*'. Some instructors thought that their only obligation was to adhere to the accommodation letter, and they were uninterested in or concerned about other opportunities to become a more inclusive instructor. The power imbalance between a professor and student, coupled with a lack of knowledge and skillset in self-advocacy, resulted in poor performance, stress, abandonment of educational aspirations, and even threats of human rights actions by SWD in my department. As a result, I began participating in one-on-one meetings between professors/session instructors and SWD. As a professor, I was able to mitigate some of the power imbalance. As a colleague, I was able to gain an instructor's attention and trust. As someone experienced in promoting inclusion and accessibility, I was able to work with SWD to articulate their needs and ideas. I was also able to offer some alternatives for the SWD to succeed.

Most of the instructors in my department have now improved their inclusive teaching practices, including offering alternative format evaluations, assignments, and tests. They also have more confidence to address students' needs directly, beyond those outlined in accommodation letters. Furthermore, the students with whom I have worked have demonstrated an improvement in their ability to advocate for themselves and gained self-confidence when interacting with other departments.

3.6.3 Teaching/Expecting Accessible Media

When teaching a continuing education course on accessible media to a diverse group of remote learners, I had to meticulously plan and prepare, as I had no prior knowledge of who would enrol in the class. Planning and testing software access, as well as determining the most effective way to communicate the course information to students, were large components of my preparation leading up to the course instruction. Given the complexity of the robust software being taught, I sought the expertise and feedback of a team of instructors and a technical support staff member to better prepare for the online rollout of a technical and hands-on class. My preparation also included steps to ensure SWD and other students had access and information to succeed in the course.

I had the opportunity to collaborate with experienced professionals from around the world and learn from their expertise. They were generous in sharing their knowledge with my students and I. One professional, Yadlovski (2023), a YouTube content creator, provided an example of how the video editing software, DaVinci, that we were using for the class could be used to produce audio description for people who are blind or have low vision. The creation of this video also had the added benefit of increasing awareness of audio description and how it can be used in the video creation process to increase accessibility within film editing practices more broadly.

A second example is when one student, who identified as being deaf in one ear, approached me with concerns that the use of regular audio equipment, such as headsets, may not be suitable due to her disability. I acknowledged her concern and responded by conducting some initial research on specialized headsets. As I was unable to find a clear solution, I consulted with the Canadian Hearing Services (CHS) organization for their advice. I connected the student with a representative from CHS and arranged a joint meeting. As I did not want the cost of a specialized headset to be another barrier, the headset was purchased by the institution for the class's use as needed. Although this student was somewhat apprehensive about the technical aspects of the course, with encouragement and follow-up on her specific concerns, she was able to complete the course and finish her assignments with excellent results.

For this course, I spent about two extra hours before class began with those who wanted to review any concerns, including accessibility or other issues, and course management and expectations. I thought that paying attention to details and addressing individual concerns helped to reduce anxieties, especially for students who had no prior experience with online courses or for those students who had been away from a school environment for some time. I do recall it was important in terms of the position in class for students who were hard of hearing and it was important for them to know if they could not hear me or other students speaking in the class.

3.7 Exercises and Questions for Reflection

3.7.1 Questions for Reflection on Past Experiences

1. Reflect on a situation in a class where a student provided an accommodation letter from the accommodation services. What did you do? How did you interact with the student to understand their needs? What could have been improved?
2. Consider a recent evaluation instrument that you have devised (e.g., a midterm test). Evaluate the cognitive and physical demands of the instrument. What alternatives could have been used for a person with a cognitive challenge? A physical challenge?

3. Consider a situation in which you used a specific technology in your classroom. How might the technology have posed a challenge for someone with a sensory, cognitive or physical disability?

3.7.2 Self-Assessment Exercises

Suggested questions for use as self-assessments or small group discussion with colleagues on inclusive teaching practices:

1. How can you be prepared for, while also, willing to be flexible to modify your teaching for a range of post-secondary students, including SWD. How can your teaching impact student's learning experience?
2. What are the legal requirements and accommodations mandated by the laws in your country or region (e.g., the Americans with Disabilities Act (ADA) and Section 504 of the Rehabilitation Act, and the Accessible Canada Act)?
3. How do you ensure that appropriate accommodations are provided to SWD in your classroom or online courses?
4. Reflect on how you collaborate with campus disability support services?
5. What elements of your course syllabi are inclusive and exclusive of SWD.
6. How can accessible course materials and resources, such as alternative formats (e.g., electronic texts, captioned videos) be made available in your course? Where can you find these?
7. What are current best practices and emerging technologies for supporting SWD in post-secondary education, where can you find them?

References

Bickenbach, J. E., Cieza, A., & Sabariego, C. (2016). Disability and public health. In *International Journal of Environmental Research and Public Health* (Vol. 13, Issue 1, p. 123). MDPI.

Boud, D., Cohen, R., & Sampson, J. (1999). Peer learning and assessment. *Assessment & Evaluation in Higher Education, 24*(4), 413–426.

Branch, L. S. (2019, July 11). *Consolidated federal laws of Canada, Accessible Canada Act*. https://laws-lois.justice.gc.ca/eng/acts/a-0.6/

Canada, E. and S. D. (2020, November 5). *Summary of the Accessible Canada Act* [Policies]. https://www.canada.ca/en/employment-social-development/programs/accessible-people-disabilities/act-summary.html

Clouder, L., Karakus, M., Cinotti, A., Ferreyra, M. V., Fierros, G. A., & Rojo, P. (2020). Neurodiversity in higher education: A narrative synthesis. *Higher Education, 80*(4), 757–778.

Costales, J., Abellana, J., Gracia, J., & Devaraj, M. (2021). A learning assessment applying Pomodoro technique as a productivity tool for online learning. *Proceedings of the 13th International Conference on Education Technology and Computers*, 164–167.

Dewsbury, B., & Brame, C. J. (2019). Inclusive teaching. *CBE—Life Sciences Education, 18*(2), fe2.

Dolmage, J. T. (2017). *Academic ableism: Disability and higher education*. University of Michigan Press.

Edwards, M., Poed, S., Al-Nawab, H., & Penna, O. (2022). Academic accommodations for university students living with disability and the potential of universal design to address their needs. *Higher Education, 84*(4), 779–799.

Finkelstein, S., Sharma, U., & Furlonger, B. (2021). The inclusive practices of classroom teachers: A scoping review and thematic analysis. *International Journal of Inclusive Education, 25*(6), 735–762.

Fujioka, K. (1998). The talking stick: An American Indian tradition in the ESL classroom. *The Internet TESL Journal, 4*(9), 1–6.

Gany, F., Kapelusznik, L., Prakash, K., Gonzalez, J., Orta, L. Y., Tseng, C.-H., & Changrani, J. (2007). The impact of medical interpretation method on time and errors. *Journal of General Internal Medicine, 22*, 319–323.

Government of Canada, D. of J. (2021, March 15). *The Canadian Charter of Rights and Freedoms*. https://www.justice.gc.ca/eng/csj-sjc/rfc-dlc/ccrf-ccdl/

Hurwitz, J. T., Elliott, S. N., & Braden, J. P. (2007). The influence of test familiarity and student disability status upon teachers' judgments of students' test performance. *School Psychology Quarterly, 22*(2), 115.

Individuals with Disabilities Education Act (IDEA). (n.d.). Individuals with Disabilities Education Act. Retrieved September 25, 2023, from https://sites.ed.gov/idea/

Kane, M. (2020). The impact of time limits and timing information on validity. In *Integrating timing considerations to improve testing practices* (pp. 19–31). Routledge.

Kaundinya, T., & Schroth, S. (2022). Dismantle ableism, accept disability: Making the case for anti-ableism in medical education. *Journal of Medical Education and Curricular Development, 9*, 23821205221076660.

Kulkarni, M. (2012). Contextual Factors and Help Seeking Behaviors of People With Disabilities. *Human Resource Development Review, 11*(1), 77–96. https://doi.org/10.1177/1534484311416488

Laitusis, C. C., Morgan, D. L., Bridgeman, B., Zanna, J., & Stone, E. (2007). EXAMINATION OF FATIGUE EFFECTS FROM EXTENDED-TIME ACCOMMODATIONS ON THE SAT REASONING TEST™. *ETS Research Report Series, 2007*(2), i–13.

Lean, Y., & Shan, F. (2012). Brief review on physiological and biochemical evaluations of human mental workload. *Human Factors and Ergonomics in Manufacturing & Service Industries, 22*(3), 177–187.

Lezzoni, L. I., Rao, S. R., Ressalam, J., Bolcic-Jankovic, D., Agaronnik, N. D., Donelan, K., Lagu, T., & Campbell, E. G. (2021). Physicians' Perceptions Of People With Disability And Their Health Care: Study reports the results of a survey of physicians' perceptions of people with disability. *Health Affairs, 40*(2), 297–306.

Li, H., Yu, J., Luo, Y., & Guo, C. (2023). Inclusion and equity: Experiences and dilemmas of disability resource centers at world-class universities. *International Journal of Chinese Education, 12*(1), 2212585X231161859.

Lovett, B. J., & Nelson, J. M. (2021). Systematic Review: Educational Accommodations for Children and Adolescents With Attention-Deficit/Hyperactivity Disorder. *Journal of the American Academy of Child & Adolescent Psychiatry, 60*(4), 448–457. https://doi.org/10.1016/j.jaac.2020.07.891

Lyman, M., Beecher, M. E., Griner, D., Brooks, M., Call, J., & Jackson, A. (2016). What keeps students with disabilities from using accommodations in postsecondary education? A qualitative review. *Journal of Postsecondary Education and Disability, 29*(2), 123–140.

Massachusetts Institute of Technology. (n.d.). *Disability and Access Services.* Disability and Access Services. https://studentlife.mit.edu/das/accommodation-procedures/students

Newman, L. A., Madaus, J. W., Lalor, A. R., & Javitz, H. S. (2021). Effect of accessing supports on higher education persistence of students with disabilities. *Journal of Diversity in Higher Education, 14*(3), 353.

Nieminen, J. H. (2022). Assessment for Inclusion: Rethinking inclusive assessment in higher education. *Teaching in Higher Education,* 1–19.

Office of the assistant secretary for administration and management. (n.d.). *Section 504, Rehabilitation Act of 1973.* U.S. Department of Labor. http://www.dol.gov/agencies/oasam/centers-offices/civil-rights-center/statutes/section-504-rehabilitation-act-of-1973

Ontario, G. of. (2005). *Accessibility for Ontarians with Disabilities Act, 2005.* http://www.e-laws.gov.on.ca/DBLaws/Statutes/English/05a11_e.htm

Rao, K., & Tanners, A. (2011). Curb cuts in cyberspace: Universal instructional design for online courses. *Journal of Postsecondary Education and Disability, 24*(3), 211–229.

Rasooli, A., Razmjoee, M., Cumming, J., Dickson, E., & Webster, A. (2021). Conceptualising a fairness framework for assessment adjusted practices for students with disability: An empirical study. *Assessment in Education: Principles, Policy & Practice, 28*(3), 301–321.

Sanger, C. S. (2020). Inclusive pedagogy and universal design approaches for diverse learning environments. *Diversity and Inclusion in Global Higher Education: Lessons from across Asia,* 31–71.

Sathy, V., & Hogan, K. A. (2019). How to make your teaching more inclusive. *The Chronicle of Higher Education, 7.*

Smith, M. R., Chai, R., Nguyen, H. T., Marcora, S. M., & Coutts, A. J. (2019). Comparing the Effects of Three Cognitive Tasks on Indicators of Mental Fatigue. *The Journal of Psychology, 153*(8), 759–783. https://doi.org/10.1080/00223980.2019.1611530

Stevens, S. (2003). Assisting the Blind and Visually Impaired: Guidelines for Eye Health Workers and Other Helpers. *Community Eye Health, 16*(45), 7–9.

Taneja-Johansson, S. (2021). Facilitators and barriers along pathways to higher education in Sweden: A disability lens. *International Journal of Inclusive Education,* 1–15.

Teach Access by Design—Teach Access. (n.d.). Retrieved July 30, 2025, from https://www.teachaccess.org/teach-access-by-design/

Toolkit, W. E. (2020, June 30). *Best Practices for Interacting with Persons with Disabilities: A Guide.* https://otc-cta.gc.ca/eng/publication/best-practices-interacting-persons-disabilities-a-guide

Toutain, C. (2019). Barriers to accommodations for students with disabilities in higher education: A literature review. *Journal of Postsecondary Education and Disability, 32*(3), 297–310.

United Nations. (2023). *The 17 Goals.* United Nations. https://sdgs.un.org/goals

University of Minnesota. (2023). *Accessibility vs. Accommodation | Accessible U.* https://accessibility.umn.edu/importance-accessibility/accessibility-vs-accommodation

Yadlovski, J. (2023). *Resolve audio & video editing* [YouTube]. Resolve Audio & Video Editing. https://www.youtube.com/c/JasonYadlovski

4 Inclusively Collecting and Analysing Data

There are numerous methods for collecting and analyzing user data. And, user data can be qualitative and/or quantitative. In Inclusive Design research, it is common to collect both types of data—mixed methods research—because recruiting enough PWD or older adults for sufficient statistical power is very difficult, and often unnecessary, particularly in qualitative research (Marshall et al. 2013). Having the unique opinions, attitudes, perspectives from users is often crucial to the research questions or objectives. Finally, generalization or transferability may not be a suitable research objective, as individual uses and differences that are necessary to ensure flexibility and customization, central principles of Inclusive Design theory, are met. Table 4.1 provides a matrix of some conventional subjective/qualitative and objective/quantitative data collection and analysis methods. While these methods can be applied in Inclusive Design research, they are often insufficient or inappropriate to use as is, requiring modifications or replacement methods in order to be accessible to the target users and to generate usable research data. In this chapter, a discussion of different considerations for collecting and analyzing data for Inclusive Design research with PWD and older adults is discussed, and alternative approaches presented.

4.1 Involving PWD and Older Adults

Collecting and analyzing data with/from users are a fundamental part of Inclusive Design research, whether university, industry or community-led research. However, decisions regarding what, when, and how to collect and analyze data can be incongruent with timelines and deliverables of a research project and/or funding programs. These factors can include recruiting a sufficient number and representative sample of target users (including

D. Fels et al., *Inclusive Design Premises, Policies, Protocols, and Practices: From Usability to Empowerment*, Synthesis Lectures on Technology and Health,
https://doi.org/10.1007/978-3-032-15746-1_4

Table 4.1 Comparison of conventional qualitative and quantitative data collection and analysis methods

Data collection	Quantitative data analysis	Qualitative data analysis
Objective (Quantitative) Numeric data that can be ordinal, interval, ratio, continuous or discrete (e.g., heart-rate, time, errors, eye movement or tracking,). Data can be collected from different sources including people	Statistical relationships and differences Example analysis methods: Parametric and non-parametric statistical analyses (t-test, ANOVA, Mann-Whitney and Kruskal-Wallace) There are numerous excellent references for statistical procedures (e.g., Privitera 2017)	Discerning and interpreting meaning from numbers Example analysis methods: Social network graphs and epidemic curves
Subjective (Qualitative) Non-numeric data such as words/text, images/ photographs, video, sound). These data can be collected from people or people-generated artefacts such as news articles or YouTube videos, using different methods such as interviews, forced-choice and open-ended questions on questionnaire/ surveys, focus groups, observation, IdeaJams, images/ photographs and video capture	Discover statistical relationships, patterns, or differences between groups/ topics/other variables Example analysis methods: Descriptive discourse analysis Descriptive statistics (mean, standard deviation, counts, frequency, etc.) Cluster analysis Graphical analysis	Discerning and interpreting meaning from patterns Example analysis methods: Grounded theory, Hermeneutics, Cultural modelling Critical discourse analysis Case study (see Miles et al. 2013 for more information on typical qualitative methods)

demographics, gender, age and education level, etc.), qualitative/quantitative data collection and analysis methods, differences between participants for user studies versus participant co-designers or co-researchers, and community-led study designs, and results interpretation, dissemination and applications. Another consideration is community-based participatory research where the concept of shared and equitable responsibility and leadership, safe and inclusive spaces, action and collaboration is critical. This type of research may also have goals and objectives that go beyond purely academic pursuits but have applied aspects as well (Benz et al. 2024; King and Gillard 2019). All of these factors must be considered through the Inclusive Design lens in order to ensure that all aspects of the research are considered inclusive, not just the recruitment of PWD. Care must also be given to how participants are recruited and to avoid using only convenience sampling techniques (Banas et al. 2019).

According to the principles of Inclusive Design, users should be considered from the beginning of the process (design, research, product development, etc.) and represent a wide range of humans (including abilities, needs and interests). Users should, thus, participate in all aspects of the research process from conceptualization to implementation. Users can be included as participant co-researchers, participant co-designers, representative study participants, evaluators, "lab" elders (where the term elder is originally a Quaker term (Malande 2019) and does not refer to an Indigenous role), community-led co-designers, data collectives and consultants. A participant co-researcher is a person who is a representative of the target user group that is involved in the research development/ project from the beginning (Bigby and Frawley 2015; Marks et al. 2018). This can involve advising as well as participating with the research team. It can also involve a professional interpreter, a care-giver, or support worker for that person. A co-researcher or lab elder can provide advice and feedback on appropriate research questions, study design, and prototype designs, as well as participate in the pilot user study(ies), data analysis, and dissemination efforts (they can often be listed as an author on manuscripts). They typically attend regular research team meetings, occupy and use physical workspaces and resources in the research facility, and interact with other research team members. A participant co-researcher is not considered a principal investigator in that they are not responsible for the research project or deliverables, but rather assist in ensuring that the user perspective is included in the development of the research. Finding participant co-researchers or designers can be a difficult task as they are being asked to provide time and interest in a specific project. Advantages for a co-researcher or designer is that there is an opportunity for greater exposure to the on-going project, being able to influence the project outcomes and advancing their own research or design skills. Advantages for the research team include access to ongoing insights rather than one-off evaluations during a single user study. The co-researcher or designer may bring novel perspectives that can change the research direction, questions or methods. Offering compensation is important for this work.

During the development of the research, data about the experience and contribution from the participant co-researcher can be collected and analyzed as part of the research process, and dissemination outcomes. A participant co-researcher could also be considered as a case study (Bigby et al. 2014) for the research. Important considerations for the participant co-researcher involve identification, confidentiality, anonymity (Tourangeau 2018) and security of the data collected from them, as well as other research ethics considerations, such as risk (Banas et al. 2019; Marks et al. 2018). An example is the reporting of a case study based on the data from a participant co-researcher, where their data are on the development of the research being reported. From a research ethics perspective, these data should be anonymized, yet their name could appear on the author list, or acknowledgement statement, but care must be taken around possible identification and affiliation with their personal lives or experiences of disability/ageing. These ethical considerations must be explicitly discussed and agreed upon with that person (including data collection, storage, disposal and issues around identification and recognition) prior to a research ethics submission.

4.1.1 Participant Co-designers

The role of participant co-designer is also common in Inclusive Design research and stems from the participatory design methodology (Hartson and Pyla 2018; Huff et al. 2020; Roberts and Pereyra 2024). A participant-co-designer fulfils a similar role as a participant co-researcher, but they are focused on the design and development of the research tools/artefacts, prototypes, objects, physical and/or computer interfaces that target users would encounter (Donoso et al. 2014; Zhu et al. 2019). They do not tend to advise on research questions, user study designs, or study instruments, such as research ethics applications, interview questions, questionnaires, etc.

4.1.2 Study Participants

Study participants are representatives from the user group(s) for whom the research is targeted. They will be involved in the application of the research method/study. For instance, they may participate in a usability study, an interview, or a longitudinal study. They will not provide input into the other aspects of the research, either early elements, such as design/development of a prototype or defining the research questions or later elements, such as analyzing the data.

4.1.3 Consultants and Evaluators

Another user position in a research project may be as a member of a research advisory or administration board. In this case, users provide overviews and general directions for the research but do not become actively involved. They may also be involved in general decision making, such as whether to take one direction or another. Finally, they are often involved in assisting with the process of recruiting study participants and disseminating study results within their communities.

All of these different types of user roles and users can be present and participate in all or select stages of the research process. For new researchers, this can be a daunting process, as recruiting users involves knowing:

- where to recruit,
- who would be available or interested,
- how to engage users with different abilities,
- when to recruit which type of user for which role(s),
- how to complete and discuss research ethics' applications,
- role implications and research methodology options, and

Fig. 4.1 Inclusive virtual meeting best practices for Zoom. Permission from Christie Christelis, 2021

- how to work with interpreters (e.g., sign language interpreters, and Deafblind intervenors) and/or carer-givers/assistants in the research (as primary, secondary, tertiary participants). Not only are the ethical implications regarding the process of interpretation and representation of the PWD, confidentiality, and differences between professional and research ethics, but there are also implications for physical space, logistics, and how to interact with these individuals in a research study context. For example, sign language interpreters or Deafblind intervenors can be required to provide signed consent as 'participants' in the research study, which may contravene their own professional ethics requirements. It is important to learn how interpreters and caregivers function, what they can and cannot do according to their professional ethics requirements, and to discuss plans for the research protocol with university or college research ethics board representatives to ensure there are appropriate ethical procedures in place for them.

While involving users in the entire research process, in general, meets one of the Inclusive Design's guiding principles, there are important details that must be considered for that involvement beyond ethics. Methods for including PWD or older adults as chair-people, or members of research meetings can involve specialized conventions and protocols that must be employed or adhered to. Never assume conventional meeting practices or technologies are accessible for all meeting members (see Fig. 4.1). Feedback from users should be obtained along the way to ensure access needs are being met and to avoid excluding individuals unknowingly. Guidelines and inclusive meeting practices exist but are difficult to obtain, understand and apply.

4.2 Designing Research Instruments, Prototypes, and Methods

4.2.1 Inclusive Methods

Research has a broad range of uses and applications, and an equally expansive range of possible methods to use at any one point in the research process. Many of these potential methods have long histories of development and distribution, with few developed or distributed from an Inclusive Design perspective. In this section, research methods for the collection and analysis of user data will be described. These can be applied at different stages of the research process, including early stage research, mid-stage/development, and for the deductive, abductive and inductive research pathways (Haig 2019; Merriam and Grenier 2019).

4.2.2 Collecting and Analyzing Data

One of the first decisions to make when beginning a user study is the target number of users to recruit. First, it depends on the research objectives or questions to answer. For example, Molich and Nielsen (1990) and Nielsen and Landauer (1993) recommend that between three and sixteen participants can identify as much as 90% of the usability issues of an interface or device (based on standardized ease of learning, ease of use, efficiency, effectiveness and satisfaction constructs). Finding problems is the main purpose of usability testing, so statistical significance or identifying common themes or theory development is not necessary.

Deriving quantitative mathematical models, such as statistically significant regression models, can require hundreds of data points or participants. In conducting user studies involving PWD and older adults, it can be difficult to recruit enough target users that meet the assumptions and requirements of parametric statistical analyses to produce generalizable models, such as linear or polynomial regression. In addition, creating generalizable statistical models tend to discount or eliminate the unique needs and perspectives of PWD that Inclusive Design purports (Adley et al. 2024; McDermott 2023; Merry 2016). It is thus rare to have research objectives related to statistical modelling in Inclusive Design research.

One common objective in Inclusive Design research is collecting qualitative data to identify prevalent factors in user perceptions, and opinions or practices for a particular issue, device, user interface, policy, social context, etc. rather than finding generalizable statistical models. This type of research objective falls into the domain of qualitative research methods, which require different participant number considerations and reasoning. Marshall et al. (2013) examined 83 articles involving studies using various qualitative methods, including Grounded Theory, single and multiple case studies, and mixed methods. They found that the majority of studies recruited between 11 and 20 participants although multiple case study research tended to have more. Clish et al. (2023) provide a scoping review of the variety of methods and reporting processes used with young PWD and participation in sport.

Mixed methods research involves combining qualitative and quantitative data collection and analysis. The subjectivity, richness and messiness of human comments, opinions, and behaviours can complement numerical data considered to be more objective and focused, but limited in scope. Quantitative data helps to answer questions about 'what', while qualitative data can help to identify the reasoning and unique nature of human interactions with the studied phenomena.

An initial assessment of user needs, ideas, existing practices, issues/problems and wishes is a common starting point in user-centred inductive research. Similar to the purpose of a literature review, where a researcher attempts to understand the research landscape involving other researchers/projects related to their particular focus, the purpose of a needs analysis is to understand the variety of user perspectives before attempting to work towards a solution to a particular identified problem. Sujan et al. (2017) identified 18 different methods for needs analysis, some of which are developed specifically for PWD. Examples of some commonly used methods include: Think Aloud Protocol with modifications for inclusion (Chandrashekar et al. 2006; Ericsson and Simon 1998; Roberts and Fels 2002); heuristic evaluation (Orozco et al. 2016), paper prototyping (Snyder 2003); Idea or Innovation Jams (Helander et al. 2007), and surveys (Andres 2012; Bosch-Baliarda et al. 2019), and some needs analysis methods specifically designed for PWD and older adults, including Cultural Probes designed for older adults (Boehner et al. 2007; Gaver et al. 1999), Show and Tell designed for older adults living with a dementia diagnosis (Astell et al. 2012; Desai and Astell 2021; Lee n.d.); and Gestural Talk Aloud Protocol designed for sign language users (Roberts and Fels 2002) and Inclusive Sensory Ethnography (Alper 2018). However, if instructions on how to implement these various methods exist, they do not often outline the suitability of the method for different types of users, or how modifications can be made for different user groups; it is up to the researcher to determine and evaluate the fit between the method and the user population.

Sujan et al. (2017) used a human abilities model to assess the fit of various needs assessment methods to various populations and then implemented this model in a methods selection tool called NICKEL. NICKEL users are asked to estimate the abilities of their potential participants along four human ability dimensions: vision, hearing, cognition and mobility. For example, the vision category encompasses sighted, low vision and blind users. NICKEL then assesses the fit of the various methods for the selected categories and offers recommendations and instructions for the suggested methods. Assessing the appropriateness of data collection methods for use in specific research using a model of user abilities, rather than just accepting a user evaluation method because it is known or well used, may provide a new and better method selection process for research involving users.

During the collection of user data beyond the initial needs analysis component, and as a result of an intervention, technological prototype testing, process evaluation, and deductive research, there are other possible methods [although there can be some overlap with needs analysis methods (e.g., survey/questionnaires, and Talk Aloud Protocols)]. Examples include participatory design (Bigby and Frawley 2015; Clemensen et al. 2007), Grounded Theory (Glaser 2017), ethnography/autoethnography (Merriam and Grenier 2019), observational and usability/user experience studies (Schwartz-Shea and Yanow 2013), and many others. This chapter will not define or explain each of these methods but readers are encouraged to seek out reference materials that explain how to apply each of the many different methods. There are fewer inclusive methods for conducting user-oriented studies compared with needs analysis methods, and this is an important gap in the inclusive research methodology area. However, one method that is not only commonly used, but also has some limited development as an inclusive method, is surveys/questionnaires. The remainder of this section will provide insights into inclusive questionnaire design and development as a research tool.

The survey or questionnaire tends to be a ubiquitous method for collecting needs, as well as, for gathering pre and post-study information from research participants. Standard question types, use of text-only (or image-only) questions and answer options, language levels, navigation with on-line tools, and paper-based questionnaires, can produce barriers for many different user types. For example, sign language users often prefer questions and answers in their signed language rather than as text. This also means that responses must be captured through a visual medium, such as video, which is unsupported in many questionnaire design tools (stand-alone, on-line or paper-based). A second example is a single switch user; as of the writing of this chapter, the author has been unable to find a questionnaire design tool where questions can be answered using a single switch/scanning system despite claims of W3C Web Content Accessibility Guideline (WGAC) compliance. Furthermore, questions themselves can also be a source of difficulty. For example, a questionnaire may be accessible to screen-reader users but it can be slow and cumbersome to keep cycling through response categories in table-type questions. Single switch users could experience similar issues with having to scan through all answer options to know the possible choices before being able to make a selection. The impact of these issues can have a significant influence on the types of questions used, as well as the design of the questionnaire instrument. In addition, most validated/standardized questionnaire instruments (e.g., SUS questionnaire—Brooke 1996) have not considered accessibility issues during their development and validity testing. These types of instruments would require modifications to make them accessible to specific audiences (e.g., reduce the literacy level of the questions) that may invalidate the instrument. As a result of the accessibility limitations of questionnaire design tools and types, use of questionnaires for specific types of users must be considered with consultations and evaluation from users. Alternative approaches, such as accessible interviews, observations or custom-coded questionnaires and response processing, may also be viable options.

Regardless of the method selected, pilot testing with actual users using their preferred access technology and/or method is important; simulation and checkers (e.g., WCAG compliance checkers) are often insufficient or miss too many factors.

4.3 Data Analysis

Once user data are collected they must then be analyzed, either qualitatively or quantitatively or both. More often than not, researchers in the Inclusive Design field must combine qualitative and relatively limited statistical analyses for quantitative data to produce credible and dependable results with smaller participant numbers, including case studies with single individuals. Statistical procedures for low number of participants (small-n) and non-normal data distribution (called non-parametric statistics), as well as, a plethora of qualitative analysis methods, are not only possible, but feasible (e.g., Gibbons and Chakraborti 2011; Norman 2010). For example, thematic analysis (Miles et al. 2013) is a common method of analyzing interview data. Interview data are coded into themes that represent the collected data. Themes can emerge from the data as an inductive procedure, or data can be coded into a pre-existing theme set, as a deductive procedure. Converting qualitative data into quantitative data, by counting the number of occurrences, allows these data points to be graphed and statistically analyzed to examine the prevalence and patterns of the interview information. Researchers must be aware, however, that frequency itself does not necessarily translate into level of importance: The theme with the highest count is not necessarily the most important. Importance can be assessed through comments from the interviews, evaluations by individuals interviewees post analysis (e.g., member checking—Birt et al. 2016), or by using other data collection methods simultaneously (e.g., inclusive questionnaire, triangulation—Creswell 2014). Similar findings from multiple methods can assist in assigning theme importance and in providing credibility to the original thematic analysis.

Non-parametric statistics, such as Mann Whitney for two independent samples, and Kruskal Wallace for more than two independent samples, are often necessary for analyzing quantitative data from small-n user studies and do not necessarily have the same interpretive power as their parametric equivalents (e.g., t-test and ANOVA). A full explanation and guide to selecting appropriate statistical tests is not within the scope of this chapter, however, there are many resources available beginning around 1957 for non-parametric statistics (Conover 1999; Hollander et al. 2013; Siegel 1957).

Another common approach for small-n studies is longitudinal and/or "within-participant" studies. Here, one participant will be involved with all aspects of the study including multiple versions of the intervention or treatment, or repeating the same tasks over multiple sessions or periods. The benefits of this type of user study include, overcoming novelty effects, understanding how people learn or become accustomed to something, and increased statistical power. But, because there is an influence on a participant's performance and perspective (due to the repeated exposure), any statistical analyses must account for these influences. Repeated measures statistics, such as the non-parametric Friedman's test (Sheskin 2003) must thus be used to account for these effects.

The process of analyzing qualitative and qualitative data can be aided by licensed and open-source software, such as NVivo™ and QDA Miner (for textual analysis), Noldus Observer™ (for video analysis), and SPSS™, and R and Python statistical libraries (for statistical analyses).

4.4 A Note on Research Ethics and Inclusive Design Research

For researchers and students associated with a university or college, any studies involving humans will require approval by a research ethics committee(s) or board(s). PWD and older adults are often considered to be vulnerable populations and ethics committees and guidelines require specialized ethics considerations in the research process (see Tri-Council Policy Statement: Ethical Conduct of Research Involving Humans—TCPS 2, Government of Canada (2023) for an example of those considerations in Canada).

To obtain ethics approval to conduct user studies with PWD and older adults, there is usually an application procedure that involves outlining the number and type of participants to be included/excluded, data collection method(s), possible risks and how they will be mitigated, as well as, consent agreement documents and all of the study instruments (e.g., questionnaires, interview questions, etc.) that will be used. The digital or paper-based consent documentation provided to participants for their agreement to participate in the study can end up being long and fairly complicated documents for participants to consume.

Some PWD and older adults may struggle with the length of and quantity of consent agreement document(s). In addition, when attempting to gain consent in the field during ad hoc recruitment where participants are approached in real time, long and complicated documents are unwieldy. Adding a one-page, point-form, accessible summary of the main ethics considerations can accompany the full detailed document so participants can more quickly gain a sense of the study and the ethical considerations.

Another issue that can arise in the ethics application process is when consent documentation/study instruments/recruitment materials must be in sign language rather than text. Most research ethics boards are unable to process sign language documents and thus a text version must also be provided. Text and sign language can be very distinct due to cultural, linguistic, and regional differences. In addition, modifications requested by the ethics board are more difficult to produce in a sign language video than a text document.

It is suggested, regardless of whether the research is Deaf or hearing, that the text documents be created first. The sign language documents can be produced once the text is approved by the ethics committee. While this does not follow an inclusive practice, it is pragmatic given the limitations of most university or hospital ethics committees and the historical exclusion of PWD in the academy.

4.5 Summary

In summary, there are many possible methods for collecting and analyzing data for Inclusive Design research. However, many existing data collection methods must be modified to be inclusive of a variety of PWD and older adults, which may invalidate the data collection instrument or introduce unplanned tasks of evaluating the method's accessibility to achieve the research objective(s). Choosing the best data collection method and accompanying data analyse methods can be a difficult and confusing task, and there is no right or wrong technique. Limitations in the recruitment process and difficulties in finding or contacting potential participants, level of method modifications required for inclusion, purpose of the research, and time and resources required will drive the data collection and analysis methods.

4.6 Exercises and Questions for Reflection

(1) Generate a 10-question questionnaire about your particular research topic, including three demographic questions. Evaluate the literacy level of the first draft using an online literacy level assessment tool. Re-work the questionnaire so that the literacy level is reduced to a grade 4 level (for a person with low literacy).

(2) Select a data collection method that you would use for your research. Evaluate the cognitive, perceptual, and motoric requirements of this method. For example, are participants required to verbalize their thoughts, use a computer keyboard and mouse or use a head-mounted display? Outline some of the issues of using that method with a blind participant. Describe what modifications must be made in order for a blind participant to be included.

References

Adley, M., Alderson, H., Jackson, K., McGovern, W., Spencer, L., Addison, M., & O'Donnell, A. (2024). Ethical and practical considerations for including marginalised groups in quantitative survey research. *International Journal of Social Research Methodology*, *27*(5), 559–574. https://doi.org/10.1080/13645579.2023.2228600

Alper, M. (2018). Inclusive sensory ethnography: Studying new media and neurodiversity in everyday life. *New Media & Society, 20*(10), 3560–3579.

Andres, L. (2012). *Designing & Doing Survey Research.* SAGE Publications, Ltd. https://doi.org/10.4135/9781526402202

Astell, A., Williams, E. A., Hwang, F., Norton, M., Adlam, T., Lethbridge, K., Wright, D., Harney-Levine, S., & Ellis, M. (2012). COBALT: Challenging obstacles and barriers to assistive living technologies. *Gerontechnology, 11*(2), 151–151.

Banas, J. R., Magasi, S., The, K., & Victorson, D. E. (2019). Recruiting and retaining people with disabilities for qualitative health research: Challenges and solutions. *Qualitative Health Research, 29*(7), 1056–1064.

Benz, C., Scott-Jeffs, W., McKercher, K. A., Welsh, M., Norman, R., Hendrie, D., Locantro, M., & Robinson, S. (2024). Community-based participatory-research through co-design: Supporting collaboration from all sides of disability. *Research Involvement and Engagement, 10*(1), 47. https://doi.org/10.1186/s40900-024-00573-3

Bigby, C., & Frawley, P. (2015). Conceptualizing inclusive research: A participatory research approach with people with intellecutal disability: Paradigm or method. *Participatory Qualitative Research Methodologies in Health,* 136–160.

Bigby, C., Frawley, P., & Ramcharan, P. (2014). A collaborative group method of inclusive research. *Journal of Applied Research in Intellectual Disabilities, 27*(1), 54–64.

Birt, L., Scott, S., Cavers, D., Campbell, C., & Walter, F. (2016). Member checking: A tool to enhance trustworthiness or merely a nod to validation? *Qualitative Health Research, 26*(13), 1802–1811.

Boehner, K., Vertesi, J., Sengers, P., & Dourish, P. (2007). How HCI interprets the probes. *Proceedings of the SIGCHI Conference on Human Factors in Computing Systems,* 1077–1086.

Bosch-Baliarda, M., Soler Vilageliu, O., & Orero, P. (2019). Toward a sign language-friendly questionnaire design. *The Journal of Deaf Studies and Deaf Education, 24*(4), 333–345.

Brooke, J. (1996). SUS: a "quick and dirty" usability scale. In *Usability evaluation in industry* (pp. 189–194). Taylor Francis.

Chandrashekar, S., Stockman, T., Fels, D., & Benedyk, R. (2006). *Using think aloud protocol with blind users: A case for inclusive usability evaluation methods. October*, 251–252.

Clemensen, J., Larsen, S. B., Kyng, M., & Kirkevold, M. (2007). Participatory Design in Health Sciences: Using Cooperative Experimental Methods in Developing Health Services and Computer Technology. *Qualitative Health Research, 17*(1), Article 1. https://doi.org/10.1177/1049732306293664

Clish, M., Enright, E., Sperka, L., & Tweedy, S. (2023). Engaging young people with disabilities in research about their experiences of physical education and sport: A scoping review of methodologies and methods. *European Physical Education Review, 29*(3), 331–350. https://doi.org/10.1177/1356336X221141598

Conover, W. J. (1999). *Practical nonparametric statistics* (Vol. 350). John Wiley & Sons.

Creswell, J. W. (2014). *Research design: Qualitative, quantitative, and mixed methods approaches.* SAGE Publications, Ltd.

Desai, S., & Astell, A. (2021). Mixed reality technologies for people with dementia: Participatory evaluation methods. *arXiv Preprint arXiv:2107.07336.*

Donoso, V., Van Mechelen, M., & Verdoodt, V. (2014). Increasing User Empowerment through Participatory and Co-design Methodologies. *KU Leuven, Leuven.* http://www.academia.edu/download/35672932/D1.3.1c_ICRI1.pdf

Ericsson, K. A., & Simon, H. A. (1998). How to study thinking in everyday life: Contrasting think-aloud protocols with descriptions and explanations of thinking. *Mind, Culture, and Activity, 5*(3), 178–186.

Gaver, B., Dunne, T., & Pacenti, E. (1999). Design: Cultural probes. *Interactions, 6*(1), 21–29.

Glaser, B. (2017). *Discovery of grounded theory: Strategies for qualitative research.* Routledge.

Gibbons, J. D., & Chakraborti, S. (2011). Nonparametric statistical inference. In *International encyclopedia of statistical science* (pp. 977–979). Springer.

Government of Canada, I. A. P. on R. E. (2023, January 11). *Tri-Council Policy Statement: Ethical Conduct for Research Involving Humans—TCPS 2 (2022).* https://ethics.gc.ca/eng/policy-politique_tcps2-eptc2_2022.html

Haig, B. D. (2019). The importance of scientific method for psychological science. *Psychology, Crime & Law, 25*(6), 527–541. https://doi.org/10.1080/1068316X.2018.1557181

Hartson, R., & Pyla, P. S. (2018). *The UX book: Agile UX design for a quality user experience.* Morgan Kaufmann.

Helander, M., Lawrence, R., Liu, Y., Perlich, C., Reddy, C., & Rosset, S. (2007). Looking for great ideas: Analyzing the innovation jam. *Proceedings of the 9th WebKDD and 1st SNA-KDD 2007 Workshop on Web Mining and Social Network Analysis*, 66–73. https://doi.org/10.1145/1348549.1348557

Hollander, M., Wolfe, D. A., & Chicken, E. (2013). *Nonparametric statistical methods* (Vol. 751). John Wiley & Sons.

Huff Jr, E. W., Lucaites, K. M., Roberts, A., & Brinkley, J. (2020). Participatory Design in the Classroom: Exploring the Design of an Autonomous Vehicle Human-Machine Interface with a Visually Impaired Co-Designer. *Proceedings of the Human Factors and Ergonomics Society Annual Meeting, 64*(1), 1921–1925.

King, C., & Gillard, S. (2019). Bringing together coproduction and community participatory research approaches: Using first person reflective narrative to explore coproduction and community involvement in mental health research. *Health Expectations, 22*(4), 701–708. https://doi.org/10.1111/hex.12908

Lee, J. (n.d.). Show and Tell. *TUNGSTEN Training.* Retrieved March 1, 2023, from http://tungsten-training.com/show-and-tell

Malande, O. L. (2019). The Concept of Hierarchy and Doing Ministry in the Church: Evaluating the Roles of Leaders and the Use of Authority in Quakerism. *Quaker Religious Thought, 133*(1), 5.

Marks, S., Mathie, E., Smiddy, J., Jones, J., & da Silva-Gane, M. (2018). Reflections and experiences of a co-researcher involved in a renal research study. *Research Involvement and Engagement, 4*, 1–10.

Marshall, B., Cardon, P., Poddar, A., & Fontenot, R. (2013). Does sample size matter in qualitative research?: A review of qualitative interviews in IS research. *Journal of Computer Information Systems, 54*(1), 11–22.

McDermott, R. (2023). On the scientific study of small samples: Challenges confronting quantitative and qualitative methodologies. *The Leadership Quarterly, 34*(3), 101675.

Merriam, S. B., & Grenier, R. S. (2019). *Qualitative Research in Practice: Examples for Discussion and Analysis.* John Wiley & Sons, Incorporated. http://ebookcentral.proquest.com/lib/ryerson/detail.action?docID=5630257

Merry, S. E. (2016). *The seductions of quantification: Measuring human rights, gender violence, and sex trafficking.* University of Chicago Press. https://www.degruyterbrill.com/document/doi/10.7208/9780226261317/html

Miles, M. B., Huberman, A. M., & Saldana, J. (2013). *Qualitative data analysis.* Sage. https://books.google.ca/books?hl=en&lr=&id=3CNrUbTu6CsC&oi=fnd&pg=PR1&dq=miles+and+huberman+qualitative+data+analysis&ots=Lh11hiVP0f&sig=AO4EafCyeIwZ0vy07cCqNI758a8

Molich, R., & Nielsen, J. (1990). Improving a human-computer dialogue. *Communications of the ACM, 33*(3), Article 3.

Nielsen, J., & Landauer, T. K. (1993). A mathematical model of the finding of usability problems. Amstredam, 206–213.

Norman, G. (2010). Likert scales, levels of measurement and the "laws" of statistics. *Advances in Health Sciences Education, 15*(5), Article 5.

Orozco, A., Tabares, V., & Duque, N. (2016). Methodology for heuristic evaluation of web accessibility oriented to types of disabilities. *Universal Access in Human-Computer Interaction. Methods, Techniques, and Best Practices: 10th International Conference, UAHCI 2016, Held as Part of HCI International 2016, Toronto, ON, Canada, July 17–22, 2016, Proceedings, Part I 10*, 91–97.

Privitera, G. J. (2017). *Statistics for the behavioral sciences.* Sage publications.

Roberts, V., & Fels, D. I. (2002). *Methods for inclusion: Employing think aloud protocol with individuals who are deaf: Vol. Linz* (K. Miesenberger Claus, J. &. Zagler, W., Ed.; pp. 284–291). Springer.

Roberts, V., & Pereyra, D. (2024). Inclusive co-research with experts with disabilities. In *Handbook of disability: Critical thought and social change in a globalizing world.* Springer Nature.

Schwartz-Shea, P., & Yanow, D. (2013). *Interpretive research design: Concepts and processes.* Routledge.

Sheskin, D. J. (2003). *Handbook of parametric and nonparametric statistical procedures.* Chapman and hall/CRC.

Siegel, S. (1957). Nonparametric statistics. *The American Statistician, 11*(3), Article 3.

Snyder, C. (2003). *Paper prototyping: The fast and easy way to design and refine user interfaces.* Morgan Kaufmann.

Sujan, J. S. S., Neumann, W. P., Fels, D. I. (2017). Human capability demands required from the elderly and disabled participants in the user centered design needs elicitation methods - a survey study. *Proceedings of 48th Annual Conference of the Association of Canadian Ergonomists, Banff*, 496–502.

Tourangeau, R. (2018). Confidentiality, privacy, and anonymity. *The Palgrave Handbook of Survey Research*, 501–507.

Zhu, R., Hardy, D., & Myers, T. (2019). Co-designing with adolescents with autism spectrum disorder: From ideation to implementation. *Proceedings of the 31st Australian Conference on Human-Computer-Interaction*, 106–116.

5 Business Models and Inclusive Design

Inclusive design is about design, development and deployment of services, and products to be inclusive of as many human abilities as possible. People with varying abilities, limitations, and disabilities are included in the design process right from the start. The development and deployment of services and products is also the purview of business and entrepreneurship in terms of delivering them to target users for remuneration. However, there is often a mismatch or lack of consideration between these two methods beginning at the design stage where specifications/ideas can be motivated by different goals such as first-to-market versus time needed to ensure inclusion, large versus small markets, assumptions about target audiences or users versus conducting a needs analysis to understand user's needs, and common business practices (Holmes 2018). While there are many guidelines, prior research, discussion and efforts at the design and organizational policy levels including business cases for inclusion (see Holmes 2018; Langdon et al. 2020; O'Donovan 2018; Sulastri et al. 2024; Waller et al. 2015; Zallio and Clarkson 2021, among many examples), there is less available to inform business initiation, development and deployment practices.

The system put in place to carry these practices out is often defined by a business model whereby the aspects of implementing the design and/or idea to the market can be simulated and justified. The business model helps outline the motivation and purpose for, economic value of, and the interconnected elements required for delivering the product or service to the marketplace.

The business model canvas proposed by Osterwalder and Pigneur (2010) is a popular and pragmatic method for identifying and describing the main elements required for a business to deliver a specific set of products or services. This model is relevant to

D. Fels et al., *Inclusive Design Premises, Policies, Protocols, and Practices: From Usability to Empowerment*, Synthesis Lectures on Technology and Health,
https://doi.org/10.1007/978-3-032-15746-1_5

inclusive design because it considers the human elements, such as customers and stakeholders, along with economic considerations. They list nine main elements for the model: Key Partners, Activities, Resources required, Value proposition, Customer relationships, Channels, Costs, Revenues and Customer segments defined by Osterwalder and Pigneur as follows:

(1) Customer segments: The target user groups at which the product or service is aimed. This can involve multiple groups of users as well as individuals with differing needs. This domain can include the presumed extrinsic and intrinsic orientation of the business to the customers and, in turn, their orientations to the business.
(2) Product/Service Value proposition: The value proposition is the explicitly justified link between the business products and/or services and the motivation to purchase them by customers. This is different from the respective orientations of the business and its customers/stakeholders that modulate how that motivation is expressed. The value proposition can be specifically directed towards solving a user's problem, satisfying a need or addressing an outstanding issue. There are six main drivers of the product/service value proposition: newness, customization, performance, pragmatics of allowing task completion, competitive pricing, status/brand, design, availability, usability, reduced risk.
(3) Channels: Channels are the mechanisms by which the organisation is connected to customers in order to drive awareness, purchases, evaluation, post-purchase customer support and deliver value. All five of these factors must be considered when identifying and defining the channels of operation in the model.
(4) Customer relationships: Defined as the types and functions of the specific relationships maintained with the various identified customer groups as part of doing business. The purpose of this element is to clearly identify how customers will be acquired, retained and boosted.
(5) Revenues: Money earned from the various customer groups and stakeholders through the development and distribution of business products/service minus the costs of doing business. More broadly it is the amount of funds customers and stakeholders are willing to invest or transfer in order for the product/service value proposition to be realized. These can be direct revenues or net-present value calculations and involves specifying how do customers and stakeholders pay for business product and distribution transactions and in what manner, and how much does each revenue stream contribute to the overall cash flow needed to keep the business operating.
(6) Key resources: Key individuals, financial, intellectual, physical, equipment, supplies, and technology required to create, produce and deliver the value proposition. These can be owned by the company, leased from a third party, offered by key partners. It can also include intangible resources that can be drawn upon from being part of a cooperative or family enterprise driven by values and orientations outside of the specific business.

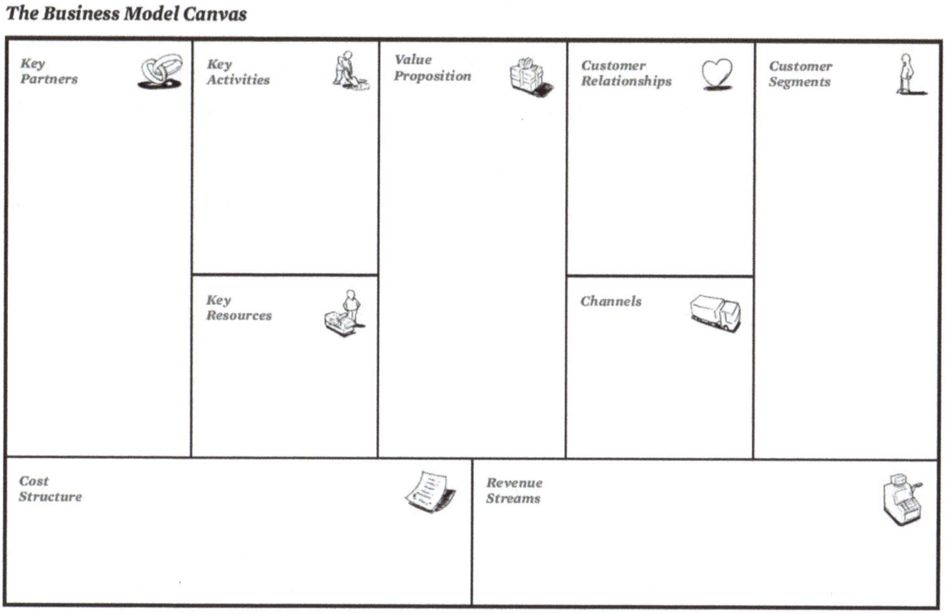

Fig. 5.1 Template for developing business model (Osterwalder and Pigneur 2010, p. 44). The template can be found at www.businessmodelgeneration.com

(7) Key activities: These are the main tasks and activities that are required to successfully deliver the value proposition to the customer segments. They can include tasks involved in production, platform or network and/or problem solving involved in creating and delivering the value proposition.
(8) Key partners: individuals, other companies, suppliers or organisations, as well as communities and others that provide resources, efficiencies, risk reduction in order to optimize the business.
(9) Costs: All of the costs involved in running the business. They are defined or quantified once Key activities, resources and partners are defined. They can be financial or non-financial in nature (e.g., includes the monetary cost of goods sold as well as reputational or branding costs).

Identifying and defining all of the nine elements contained within the business model canvas is an important aspect of creating a business model to describe the idea, motivation and structure of business. It is also important to understand the relationship between these elements. (Osterwalder and Pigneur 2010) provide a visual template to identify the elements as well as how they are related to each other (see Fig. 5.1). Creating a business model canvas then involves populating the nine elements with carefully thought through considerations and iterations to ensure completeness and priorities for the business.

As shown in Fig. 5.1, the typical business model canvas is focused on what is required to drive the economic level of the business and is a 2-dimensional perspective of a business (Joyce and Paquin 2016). Other aspects of a business that have become more important in today's climate of environmental protection and social responsibility have motivated business model experts to add new layers to the basic canvas to allow for expanded elements and reflect that multi-dimensionality that constitute most businesses. They also act to guide the management of these elements of the business that are not directly related to the primary transactions defining the business. For example, Joyce and Paquin (2016) added environmental life cycle and social layers to the basic template that provide horizontal and vertical correspondence to the overall model (see Fig. 5.2).

5.1 Business Canvas—Inclusive Design

Building on the multi-layer, multi-dimensional business model canvas proposed by Joyce and Paquin (2016) it is possible to consider other layers that can influence business direction, strategy and implementation through the lens of inclusive design. This perspective can add another layer to the business canvas in order to integrate it into the fold of business thinking and planning. Figure 5.3 presents the concepts of inclusive design that correspond to each of the nine business canvas model economic elements and defined as follows:

(1) Target User Groups, Orientations, Expectations and Fit: This element involves identifying and specifying the widest possible range of users. Rather than naming groups of people such as those who are Blind and attempting to know and understand all of the different types of individuals, identifying the ranges of human abilities for vision, hearing, motor and cognitive, social and expectations of an increasingly segmented definition of users for which a design must work will simplify the process of designing for accommodations. Understanding issues that can occur with designs as a result of limitations in human abilities can assist in informing product designs anticipated to satisfy the core business value proposition for a plurality of people all recognized as being valid customers who need to be accommodated. Matching abilities and preferences with design functionality and human interfaces can assist in informing design (Bound and Coleman 2005). Tools and techniques that support this matching process can be used (Zitkus et al. 2013). Standards and regulations influence the legal and public expectations designing inclusively. A final consideration that we have found to be useful is to consider interface designs that can satisfy the ends of the normal distribution curve rather than the centre/average.

(2) Inclusive Design Value: ID value arises when design has an impact on positive product and economic outcomes and avoids negative results from legal or standards challenges. ID value is obtained through greater understanding of user needs and abilities

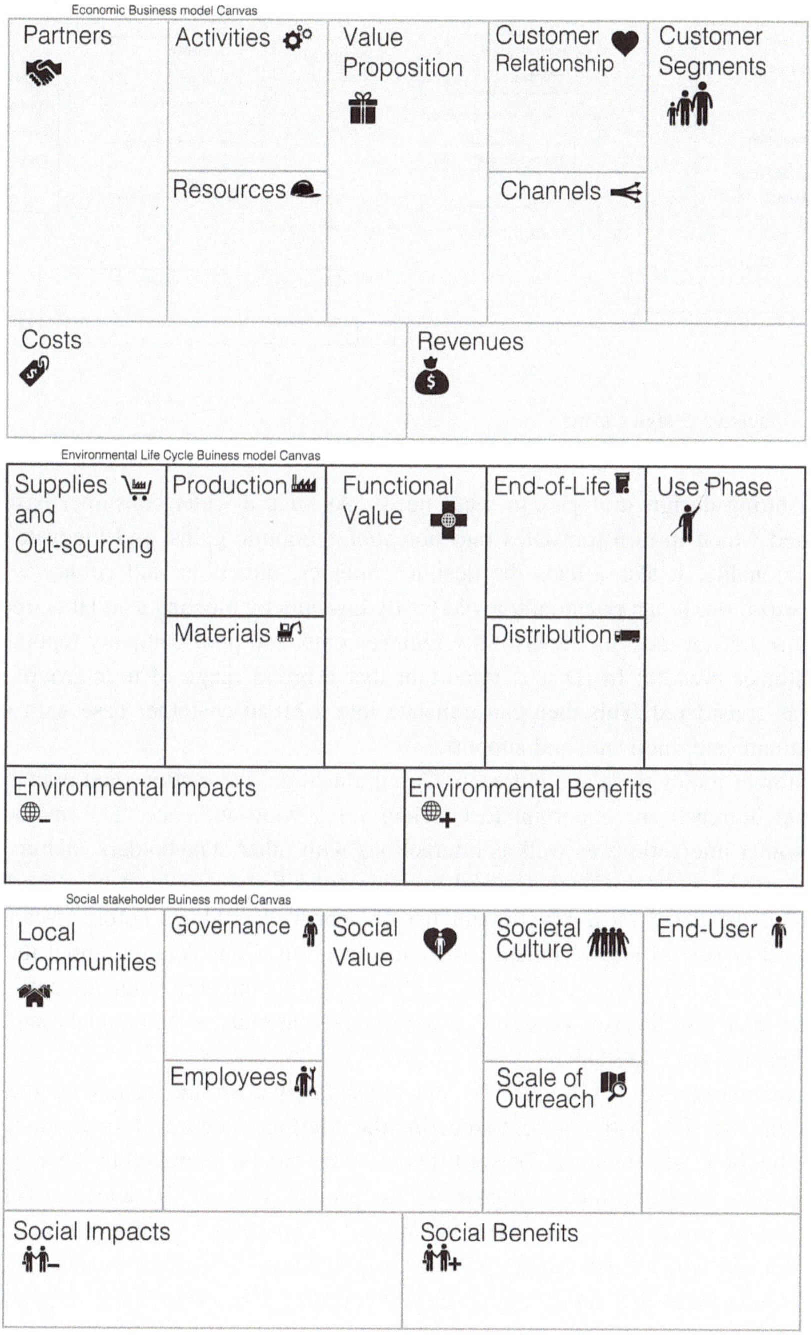

Fig. 5.2 Environmental and social layers that complement and integrate with the economic layer of the business model canvas

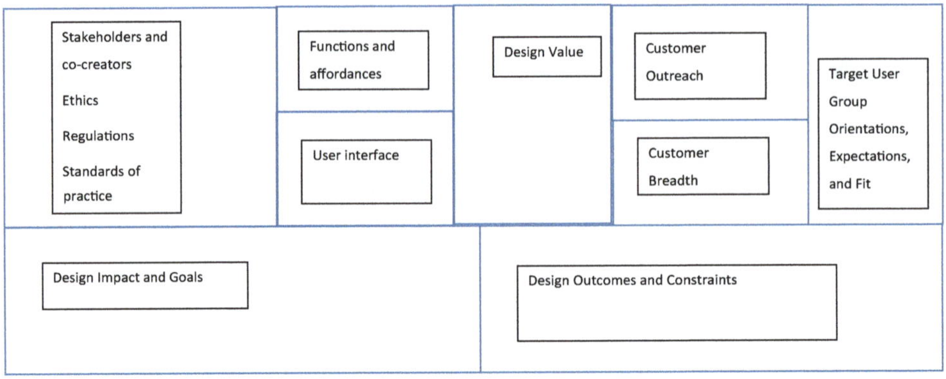

Fig. 5.3 Inclusive design canvas

and fitting design strategies to these needs. As such a wider consumer base is supported which in turn translates into potential economic gains, and innovate designs/functionality. It also affects the design strategies, directions and culture within the organization. It can potentially avoid costly lawsuits by meeting standards, retrofitting as a result not meeting accessibility requirements, and poor company reputation.

(3) Customer breadth: In ID it is important that a broad range of user groups s possible is considered. This then can translate into a broad customer base with which to communicate, motivate, and support.

(4) Customer interactions and outreach: Communication, interactions and managing customer outreach are important to consider for a wide audience. This include direct customer interactions as well as interactions with other stakeholders such as parents, support organizations/agencies and governments. For example, a new product may need to be listed on a government list of approved products before it can be purchased as part of a government assistance program. Consideration about the options for outreach must also be inclusive. For example, having sign language options, large print, and low literacy versions of marketing materials, user manuals and support documents are important.

(5) ID outcomes and constraints: ID outcomes revolve around achieving the desired design objectives with respect to meeting the interface access and functionality identified by the target audience. Desired ID outcomes can be identified in the specification process or in determining the goals of the project. Because ID does not necessarily address all levels and types of human abilities as possible, identifying which levels of ability and which functionality will not be considered is a part of understanding and making explicit the limitations of the ID process. This element involves evaluating of whether design outcomes meet expectations and achieve design objectives through frequent inclusive end user testing (Langdon et al. 2014) and co-design (Donoso et al. 2014; Jones 2018; Strokosch and Osborne 2020) with a variety of user partners as

identified in Element 1 that occurs throughout the design process, from beginning to end. Inclusive evaluation methodologies (Maragiannis et al. 2019; Sujan et al. 2017) would be employed.

(6) Functions: Identifying which functions are required or desirable of any design is a standard method of specifying a project or business. This are often listed in a specification document or business mandate. Applying an inclusive design lens to this element necessitates that ID considerations for additional functionality or alternative functionality are outlined.

(7) User interface, metaphors and affordances: The user interface consists of all of the aspects of an entity (product, design, business) with which a user interacts; often called front-facing (Preece et al. 2015). This aspect of the business or product can be outlined in specification or business description documents. Adherence to legislation, such as the Accessibility for Ontarians with Disability Act (Ontario 2005), the Accessible Canada Act (*Government Bill (House of Commons) C-81 (42–1)—Royal Assent—Accessible Canada Act—Parliament of Canada* n.d.) or the American with Disabilities Act, and regulations such as the Canadian Radio, Television and Telecommunication Commission regulations (e.g., (C. R. and T. C. (CRTC) Government of Canada 2008a, 2008b) or the Web Content Accessibility Guidelines (*Web Content Accessibility Guidelines (WCAG) 2.1* n.d.-b) regarding the necessities for inclusion and accessibility are necessary for ID. Best practices in inclusive design for user interfaces can also guide the specification exercise. Designing for these bottom and top sectors of the normal distribution curve for human abilities drives innovation and new design thinking as it challenges conventional practices. Affordances (Gaver 1991; Gibson 1977; Kose 1998) relate to taking advantage of the natural or innate appearance of an entity (object, design or business) communicates its function or purpose. Metaphors or analogies relate to using a similarity with another entity to communicate its purpose and take advantage of user's knowledge and/or experience with that entity (Preece et al. 2015, Lakoff and Johnson 1980). A final aspect of the user interface element is the identification and documentation of interaction language, terminology and descriptions of the various interface constructs to enable learning, transference from other user experiences and standards, and understanding by the target users.

(8) Stakeholders, ethics and regulations act as motivators, drivers and considerations for the business. Stakeholders are those individuals or groups who are prospective users who show interest in the products or services being offered. For example, advocacy groups, occupational therapists, government agencies and policies, parents of children in the target user group, and persons with disabilities could all be considered stakeholders. In addition, important non-human considerations are the applicable standards, regulations, legislation and ethical considerations that influence business development and decisions. For example, the accessibility standards outlined in the W3C's Web

Content Accessibility Guidelines (https://www.w3.org/TR/WCAG21/) can guide website or web application development. The Americans with Disabilities Act (https://www.ada.gov/) can guide product development.

(9) ID impact and goals: ID impact and goals represents design intention and strategy at the organizational level that are evaluated in the design outcomes element.

Stakeholders, Ethics and Regulations, and Design Value involve sense-making, and justification activities and elements. Operational and pragmatic elements are composed of the center elements of User Interface, Functions and Affordances, Customer Outcomes, Customer Breadth, and Design Outcomes and Constraints. The far upper right element of Target User Groups and Fit is related to pragmatic evaluation. Design Outcomes and Constraints also represents the design architecture and possibilities. There is overlap between Design Outcomes and Constraints with Design Impact and Goals so that some evaluation objectives and measures relate to assessing whether Design Goals were met and the resulting impact aligns with the desired impact.

5.2 Case Example: Audio Description, Audio Books and Podcasting

Audio description is designed to provide access to visual content contained in television, film, theatre, museums, walking tours, etc. for people who are blind or low vision (B/LV). It is a second audio track that provides descriptions of the important visual elements during instances when there is no dialogue. It is often short duration (less than 4 s) and uses styling and vocabulary that fits with the show or event. Prepared audio description for produced shows, repeated live shows, museum tours, etc. often can be prepared in advance using a script, multiple-takes, and voiced recordings. For live performances or shows, there is little opportunity for preparatory work other than research and rehearsal. Currently, audio description is not generated or considered at the beginning of a production process nor is it supervised by the creative team responsible for the show's production, which violates the tenets of inclusive design (Udo and Fels 2009). Udo and Fels (2010) suggest that if audio description is designed from the beginning by the original creators of the show, it would better fit in an inclusive design framework. Here, we also suggest that if audio description followed an inclusive design framework, it could reach and benefit a broader audience such as drivers or subway goers or others whose eyes are otherwise occupied.

The audio book and podcast industries are booming (Ramamurthy and Mamuwala 2024; Rowe 2019; Stewart et al. 2019) for sighted, blind and low vision audiences who prefer to listen to books/digital content rather than read them. Imagine drawing on this analogy to bring television, film, and theatre to these same audiences. As such, we propose a business canvas for this purpose (see Fig. 5.4).

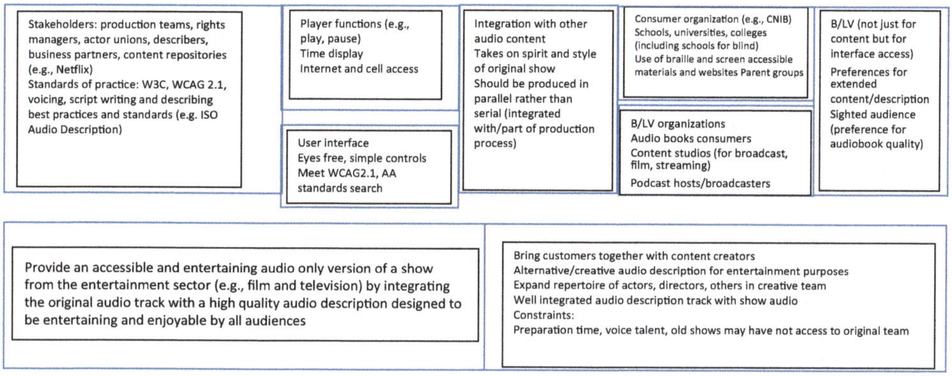

Fig. 5.4 Inclusive design canvas for audio-only television, film and theatre productions

5.3 Exercises and Questions for Reflection

1. How could inclusive design be integrated into other business models?
2. How does having an inclusive design layer in a business canvas change the financial aspects of the original business canvas?
3. Think of an existing business, or product/service line of an existing business that might benefit from having an inclusive design layer. Create one for that business.
4. Create a business canvas for a new business and apply an inclusive design layer to it, and provide an explanation of the elements you added in each box. How does this change your thinking about the business? Did you discover something unanticipated? If so, explain.
5. What are the possible overlaps with the other proposed layers (social/environmental)?

References

Bound, J., & Coleman, R. (2005). Commercial advantage from inclusive design. *Design Management Review, 16*(3), 56–63.

Donoso, V., Van Mechelen, M., & Verdoodt, V. (2014). Increasing User Empowerment through Participatory and Co-design Methodologies. *KU Leuven, Leuven.* http://www.academia.edu/download/35672932/D1.3.1c_ICRI1.pdf

Gaver, W. W. (1991). Technology affordances. *Proceedings of the SIGCHI Conference on Human Factors in Computing Systems*, 79–84.

Gibson, J. J. (1977). The theory of affordances. *Hilldale, USA, 1*(2).

Government Bill (House of Commons) C-81 (42–1)—Royal Assent—Accessible Canada Act—Parliament of Canada. (n.d.). Retrieved October 21, 2019, from https://www.parl.ca/DocumentViewer/en/42-1/bill/C-81/royal-assent

Government of Canada, C. R. and T. C. (CRTC). (2008a, December 11). *TV Access for People who are Deaf or Hard of Hearing: Closed Captioning* [Consumer information]. https://crtc.gc.ca/eng/info_sht/b321.htm

Government of Canada, C. R. and T. C. (CRTC). (2008b, December 12). *TV Access for People with Visual Impairments: Described Video and Audio Description* [Consumer information]. https://crtc.gc.ca/eng/info_sht/b322.htm

Holmes, K. (2018). *Mismatch: How inclusion shapes design.* Mit Press. https://books.google.ca/books?hl=en&lr=&id=KzNwDwAAQBAJ&oi=fnd&pg=PR7&dq=mismatch+holmes&ots=nzzalaS7ut&sig=jktQdBpap7h8pyhKe9NwoBHtLvs

Jones, P. (2018). Context of Co-Creation: Designing with System Stakeholders. In *Systemic Design: Theory, Methods and Practice: Vol. Translatonal Systems Sciences Series.* Springer Japan.

Joyce, A., & Paquin, R. L. (2016). The triple layered business model canvas: A tool to design more sustainable business models. *Journal of Cleaner Production, 135*, 1474–1486.

Kose, S. (1998). From barrier-free to universal design: An international perspective. *Assistive Technology, 10*(1), 44–50.

Lakoff, G., & Johnson, M. (1980). The metaphorical structure of the human conceptual system. *Cognitive Science, 4*(2), 195–208. https://doi-org.ezproxy.lib.torontomu.ca/10.1207/s15516709cog0402_4

Langdon, P. M., Lazar, J., Heylighen, A., & Dong, H. (2014). *Inclusive Designing: Joining Usability, Accessibility, and Inclusion.* Springer.

Langdon, P., Lazar, J., Heylighen, A., & Dong, H. (Eds.). (2020). *Designing for Inclusion: Inclusive Design: Looking Towards the Future.* Springer International Publishing. https://doi.org/10.1007/978-3-030-43865-4

Maragiannis, A., Kennedy, S., Rehal, K., & Maffioletti, C. (2019). Co-Design Methods towards Inclusive design in Diverse Communities: Empowering Youth through Entrepreneurial Skills. *Design Research for Change*, 118–119.

O'Donovan, D. (2018). Diversity and Inclusion in the Workplace. In *Organizational Behaviour and Human Resource Management* (pp. 73–108). Springer, Cham. https://doi.org/10.1007/978-3-319-66864-2_4

Ontario, G. of. (2005). *Accessibility for Ontarians with Disabilities Act, 2005.* http://www.e-laws.gov.on.ca/DBLaws/Statutes/English/05a11_e.htm

Osterwalder, A., & Pigneur, Y. (2010). *Business model generation: A handbook for visionaries, game changers, and challengers.* John Wiley & Sons.

Preece, J., Rogers, Y., & Sharp, H. (2015). *Interaction design: Beyond human-computer interaction* (Fourth). John Wiley & Sons Ltd.

Ramamurthy, S., & Mamuwala, A. (2024). Podcast Journalism. In S. Dahiya & K. Trehan (Eds.), *Handbook of Digital Journalism: Perspectives from South Asia* (pp. 351–363). Springer Nature. https://doi.org/10.1007/978-981-99-6675-2_30

Rowe, Adam. (2019, July 16). U.S. Audiobook Sales Neared $1 Billion In 2018, Growing 25% Year-Over-Year. *Forbes.* https://www.forbes.com/sites/adamrowe1/2019/07/16/us-audiobook-sales-neared-1-billion-in-2018-growing-25-year-over-year/#6c1d473a6050

Stewart, Duncan, Casey, Mark, & Wiggington, Craig. (2019, December). The ears have it: The rise of audiobooks and podcasting. *Deloitte Insights.* https://www2.deloitte.com/us/en/insights/industry/technology/technology-media-and-telecom-predictions/2020/rise-of-audiobooks-podcast-industry.html

Strokosch, K., & Osborne, S. P. (2020). Debate: If citizen participation is so important, why has it not been achieved? *Public Money & Management, 40*(1), 8–10.

Sujan, J. S. R., Neumann, W. P., & Fels, D. I. (2017). *Human capability demands required from the elderly and disabled participants in the user centred design needs elicitation methods—A survey study.*

Sulastri, R., Janssen, M., Van de Poel, I., & Ding, A. (2024). Transforming towards inclusion-by-design: Information system design principles shaping data-driven financial inclusiveness. *Government Information Quarterly, 41*(4), 101,979.

Udo, J. P., & Fels, D. I. (2009). The rogue poster-children of universal design: Closed captioning and audio description. *Journal of Engineering Design. Journal Article.* http://www.informaworld.com/smpp/content~db=all~content=a916629020

Udo, J. P., & Fels, D. I. (2010). Enhancing the entertainment experience of blind and low-vision theatre-goers through touch tours. *Disability and Society, 25*(2), 231–240.

Waller, S., Bradley, M., Hosking, I., & Clarkson, P. J. (2015). Making the case for inclusive design. *Applied Ergonomics, 46*, 297–303.

Web Content Accessibility Guidelines (WCAG) 2.1. (n.d.). Retrieved October 17, 2019, from https://www.w3.org/TR/WCAG21/

Zallio, M., & Clarkson, P. J. (2021). Inclusion, diversity, equity and accessibility in the built environment: A study of architectural design practice. *Building and Environment, 206*, 108352.

Zitkus, E., Langdon, P., & Clarkson, P. J. (2013). Inclusive Design Advisor: Understanding the Design Practice Before Developing Inclusivity Tools. *Journal of Usability Studies, 8*(4).

6 Development Practices and Implementation

The genuine desire to become an inclusive researcher, designer, educator, practitioner and business is an excellent beginning towards inclusive thinking. However, implementing and applying inclusive practices are not simple nor are they necessarily obvious. Transferring inclusive technologies and practices to the marketplace is not only difficult, but there is often an argument about PWD representing small markets that deters financial investment and business development. Also, the world is changing rapidly and updates to this thinking requires vigilance and thoughtfulness.

A recent example of a new technology is viable artificial intelligence (AI) for text- and image-based interactions. Computers are powerful enough and there are vast quantities of corpora freely available from which to draw sufficient data for the training and operation of various types of artificial intelligence systems. However, these data tend to exclude alternatives such as sign languages, or dysarthric speech as there are insufficient samples resulting in PWD being lost, under or unrepresented in these systems (see OCADU n.d.—We Count project at OCADU). Research on using AI for specialized sign language recognition and translation exists (Chattopadhyay et al. 2022; Papastratis et al. 2021; *Signapse AI|Breaking Barriers with Our AI Sign Language Translator* n.d.), but often the sample size is comparatively small, has limited condition variation such as lighting conditions, faces, bodies, and backgrounds, and/or requires complicated capture techniques such as multiple cameras, or specialized 3-D detection hardware.

Nam et al. (2020) developed an AI system, called CAIS, for automatically assessing the subjective quality of real-time closed captioning from Deaf and Hard of Hearing (D/HoH) perspectives. In order to produce sufficient data for CAIS, they used two levels of data, modelled and from actual users. Signal detection theory was used to model a Deaf and a Hard of Hearing user based on actual quality rating data from about 75 D/HoH users (Nam

D. Fels et al., *Inclusive Design Premises, Policies, Protocols, and Practices: From Usability to Empowerment*, Synthesis Lectures on Technology and Health,
https://doi.org/10.1007/978-3-032-15746-1_6

and Fels 2019). This model was then used to generate sufficient quantity of "synthetic" data (about 100,000 data points) to train and seed CAIS. In order to further allow CAIS to fine-tune its quality assessments, they used an Active Learning (Monarch 2021) process with 30 D/HoH users to agree or disagree with CAIS' assessments for 20, 15–29 s closed captioning samples. This process of modelling D/HoH assessment characteristics based on smaller numbers of actual people, which can then be used to generate sufficient data for an AI system provides an example of how PWD can be represented as a corpus.

A second concern is that the data representing PWD may be considered as outliers and ignored or removed from data sets thus perpetuating the notion of serving the majority or average (L'heureux et al. 2017). But, considering one person's needs and abilities that appear at the margins of a population distribution may benefit many others within that distribution, and result in unforeseen innovation and solutions. For example, developing a mobile phone app that includes people who are single-switch users (see Koester and Simpson 2014 for definition), considered an extreme user type, will likely result in a more accessible and usable app for many more users beyond the single-switch user.

Not only does an inclusive thinker attempt to use as many of the guidelines and best practices outlined in the inclusive design literature and discussed in previous chapters but also needs to go beyond that and ask questions such as: (1) What are challenges of applying these guidelines in a specific context?; (2) Where are the gaps?; and (3) How do I convince others of the benefits? Common guidelines for implementation include:

(1) Employing PWD in the process from the beginning, not just as evaluators but as designers, developers as well as evaluators;
(2) Evaluating with users on an on-going and continuous basis;
(3) Becoming familiar with and use applicable existing guidelines such as W3C web accessibility guidelines (*Web Content Accessibility Guidelines (WCAG) 2.1* n.d.-a) and many others (Inclusive Design Research Centre n.d.b; Joyce 2022), etc.);
(4) Learning about inclusive design;
(5) Embedding inclusive design in all endeavours such as coding, documentation, interface design, face-to-face and virtual protocols, and teaching/training; and
(6) Carrying out design audits with PWD/target users and stakeholders to ensure inclusive practices are being followed and maintained.

From a business point of view, using inclusive thinking throughout the process without the need to design exclusively for specialized markets can result in all products and services becoming inclusive; the lack of profitability arguments then evaporates. Evidence of how inclusive thinking has occurred in business can be found in mobile phone operating system designs. Examining either the Android™ or iOS™ mobile operating environments provide ample examples of how inclusive design has been integrated into the overall design of the product. First, a variety of "accessibility features and libraries" are available as a default. For example, screen colours can be modified. Text can be manipulated for different sizes, colours, transparency, etc. There are screen reader functions, VoiceOver for iOS and Navigator for TalkBack, magnifiers, text to speech or hands-free operation, single switch functionality, reduced on-screen distractions, real-time closed captioning, integration with a Braille display, hearing aid support, etc. However, many of these default features in the operating system can be overridden, intentionally or unintentionally, when developing mobile phone apps so that third party apps may exclude completely or partially those for whom this functionality was designed. An example from one research project involving single-switch users that wanted access to a specific e-book reader app demonstrated this issue. In this project, single-switch access was unavailable or failed for some, but not all, of the e-book reader functions, including the button for read aloud. As a result, the single-switch user who had low vision was unable to use that e-book reader app even though single-switch access was a default function of the iOS and Android operating systems.

One conclusion from this example is that even though default functionality is available, attention must be paid to ensuring that this functionality can still work with any new code or app for Android or iOS mobile phones. An accessibility audit and testing of computer code with the various accessibility features can assist in finding occurrences of rogue code.

While there are numerous guidelines, including those in this chapter, that provide recommendations from a more technical perspective on implementation, guidelines for the business side of implementation or transfer to the marketplace tend to be more limited. Fels and Gedeon (2011) find that entrepreneurs in the assistive technology (AT) sector tend to be social entrepreneurs (Morris et al. 2021) that are motived by customer service, and helping society and PWD rather than profit. AT businesses also are usually small niche businesses that are high risk and earnings are low. A business focused only on inclusive products and services likely must be willing to accept higher risks and lower profits in exchange for the greater good.

AT are technologies designed to support specific groups of PWD (Khasnabis et al. 2015), for example, a screen-reader (Göransson 2019) used by people who are blind to access digital materials. Inclusive design often incorporates AT into the design process for inclusive products and services, such as that described for mobile operating systems.

Regardless of the type of entrepreneurial venture and its motivation (e.g., for-profit, social, or non-profit), funding, "sweat" equity (Baecker 2023) as well as the intellectual property are all required to implement inclusive goods and services. Financing development, and marketing, sales and distribution tasks are very important entrepreneurial aspects of implementation. Investment can be difficult to acquire as there are limited sources (e.g., venture capital, angel investors, crowd-funding, bank/loans, personal savings, and family and friends), and investors are often unfavourable to limited market reach and/or projected sales due to the high-risk nature of new products and services, although there can be altruistic motivations in the crowd-sourcing model of funding (Di Pietro et al. 2018). Investors are not necessarily that interested in "good" ideas, rather they are motivated by monetary return-on-investment; even "mom and dad" want their investment back (Shane 2008). Convincing investors and the marketplace of the value of inclusive goods and services can be a daunting task. There are, however, government programs and accelerators that can provide limited start-up funding, but ultimately it is the marketplace that must be courted. Looking to governments, schools, hospitals and other public institutions as potential markets to provide acceptance and funding can take many years so relying on them exclusively may not be feasible.

One of the potential outcomes of Inclusive Design practices is that the resulting products and/or services may be beneficial, usable and useful to a wide population; PWD form only part of that wider group. It is important to understand the wider implications of inclusive products and services—considerations are to think broadly about:

(1) Who are all the possible audiences that could benefit from these products or services?
(2) What are the benefits to each of these possible target audiences?
(3) How can these benefits be realized?

Chapter 5 provides some guidance on creating an inclusive business plan, which is a good beginning to creating a "pitch" for investment and for addressing these considerations. However, these exercises are purely speculative until you summon the courage and "go for it."

6.1 The Case of the Onscreen Keyboard

The onscreen or virtual keyboard is now a familiar interface that is coupled with touch screen technologies on most smartphones, tablets, and other mobile devices. An onscreen keyboard appears on the screen for text entry whereby touching the letters/symbols on the screen selects them. It often includes word prediction that occurs as the user begins typing where the system provides a set of possible words that begin with the letters typed, which are fined tuned as more letters are entered or more context appears (Garay-Vitoria and Abascal 2006). Methods and models for word prediction vary and with more recent advances in artificial intelligence have become increasingly sophisticated and accurate (e.g., see for a description of the various models of word prediction, please see Garay-Vitoria and Abascal 2006; Lehmann et al. 2023).

Computer-based onscreen keyboards and word prediction were originally developed as an assistive technology for people with severe physical disabilities, those who could only operate a single voluntary action as an input (Thomas 1981). A set of options were displayed onscreen for the users, which were offered one at time by the system, called scanning. The first scanning method was row-column (see Fig. 6.1f), however, other techniques, such as quartering, have been developed in an attempt to increase typing efficiency. When the desired option appears, the user selects that option by activating some form of single action, e.g., pressing a switch. Childress et al. (1975) and the Tufts Interactive Communicator (Thomas 1981) created some of the first onscreen keyboards with a computer display using either dedicated hardware or the Apple II computer system. Figure 6.1a–f shows some examples of onscreen-scanning keyboards.

For single switch/scanning users, text entry rates are very slow; without word prediction results in a rate of about five words per minute or less (Koester and Simpson 2014, 2019). Using word predication can increase text entry rates to about 8–12 words per minute using a common on-screen keyboard, row/column array where the word prediction options are presented in the first row, and prediction algorithms (Alm et al. 1992; Garay-Vitoria and Abascal 2006; Todman 2000; Todman et al. 2008; Trnka et al. 2007). Word prediction combined with onscreen keyboards for scanning users has the potential to not only affect text entry time but also reduce fatigue, frustration and physical effort becoming more efficient for these users.

The efficiency gains with word prediction experienced by mobile device users not using scanning have been shown to be dependent on the text-entry expertise of the user (Arnold et al. 2020) where experienced users have little or detrimental effects of using prediction. Word length and accuracy of the prediction model are also factors in determining advantages and disadvantages of word prediction for mobile device users (Lehmann et al. 2023; Quinn and Zhai 2016). However, other benefits regardless of impact on speed have been reported such as lower cognitive load, physical or mental effort (Quinn and Zhai 2016), and improved composition (Arnold et al. 2020; Lehmann et al. 2023).

As demonstrated in this brief example and about 20 years of technological advances, what began as a computer-based communication aid for people living with severe physical disabilities has become a widely accepted and used technology for many users of mobile devices. The onscreen keyboards on mobile devices have reduced functionality and is considerably simplified compared with those used for scanning users (see Fig. 6.1d, f) but the basic keyboard layout is similar. Industry and researchers are continuing to carry research and development that will improve the efficiency and usefulness of the onscreen keyboard for many different types of users.

6.2 Exercises and Questions for Reflection

(1) Carry out a survey of businesses focused on Inclusive Design products and services as well as those focused on Assistive Technologies. Classify them into for-profit and non-profit/social type businesses, and small, medium and large enterprises (you will find definitions of these types of businesses in the literature). What types of inclusive products and services do these companies sell.

(2) Determine how much "sweat equity", and funding would be required for the business case developed from Chap. 5. Identify possible sources of funding and how they can be approached.

a

b

c

Fig. 6.1 **a** Tufts interactive communicator (Foulds 1976). Image from (Vanderheiden 2022). **b** Apple II with onscreen scanning keyboard and word prediction Image from (Mystère n.d.) licensed under the Creative Commons Attribution-Share Alike 3.0 Unported License (https://creativecommons.org/licenses/by-sa/3.0/deed.en). **c** ScreenType by Personics for the MacIntosh computer, 1986 (Anson 1991). Image from: Microsoft n.d. **d** WiVik™ on-screen keyboard with scanning for people with physical disabilities. First introduced in 1991 (*From Holland Bloorview to Berkeley Castle* n.d.). Image from Prenke-Romich (2009). **e** My-T-Mouse software—on-screen scanning keyboard (2023). Image from: (*My-T-Mouse Software—on-Screen Keyboards, Etc.* n.d.). **f** Original on-screen keyboard (no word prediction) for messaging app for first Apple iPhone released in June 2007 (from *Look Back at CNET's Original iPhone Review* n.d.)

d
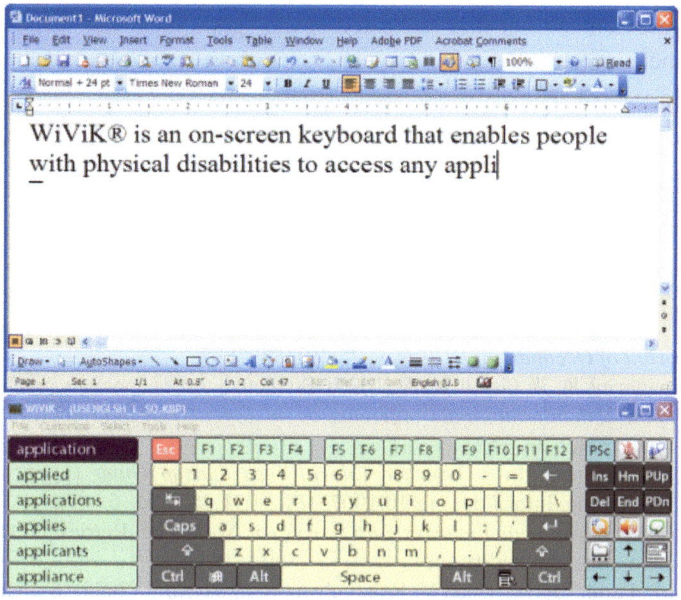

e
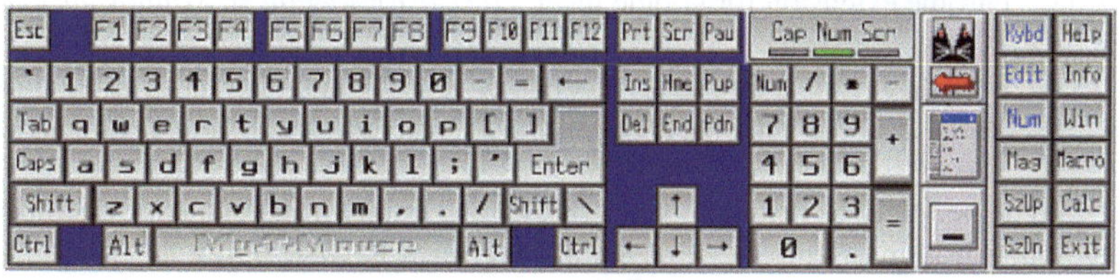

f

Fig. 6.1 (continued)

(3) Develop a 10-slide "pitch or slide deck" for approaching potential funders. Be mindful that most investors are not that interested in the "good idea" but would like to see a return on their investment.

References

Alm, N., Arnott, J. L., & Newell, A. F. (1992). Prediction and conversational momentum in an augmentative communication system. *Communications of the ACM*, *35*(5), Article 5.

Anson, D. (1991). Using the Headmaster with Macintosh, Apple II, and MS-DOS computers. *The American Journal of Occupational Therapy*, *45*(10), 889–897.

Arnold, K. C., Chauncey, K., & Gajos, K. Z. (2020). Predictive text encourages predictable writing. *Proceedings of the 25th International Conference on Intelligent User Interfaces*, 128–138. https://doi.org/10.1145/3377325.3377523

Baecker, R. (2023). Finances. In R. Baecker, *Ethical Tech Startup Guide* (pp. 85–99). Springer International Publishing. https://doi.org/10.1007/978-3-031-18780-3_6

Centre, I. D. R. (n.d.). *Creating an inclusive data ecosystem.* We Count. Retrieved October 3, 2023, from https://main--wecount.netlify.app/

Chattopadhyay, M., Parulekar, M., Bhat, V., Raisinghani, B., & Arya, S. (2022). Sign language translation using a chrome extension for google meet. *2022 IEEE Region 10 Symposium (TENSYMP)*, 1–5.

Childress, D. S., Kaplan, J. M., & Strysik, J. S. (1975). A unified approach to communications and control for severely disabled persons. *Devices and Systems for the Disabled, Philadelphia*, 197–201.

Di Pietro, F., Prencipe, A., & Majchrzak, A. (2018). Crowd Equity Investors: An Underutilized Asset for Open Innovation in Startups. *California Management Review*, *60*(2), 43–70. https://doi.org/10.1177/0008125617738260

Fels, D. I., & Gedeon, S. A. (2011). Understanding motivations of entrepreneurs in the assistive technology market. *Technology and Disability*, *23*(2), 53–64.

Foulds, R. A. (1976). *The Tufts Non-Vocal Communication Program.* https://eric.ed.gov/?id=ED138003

Garay-Vitoria, N., & Abascal, J. (2006). Text prediction systems: A survey. *Universal Access in the Information Society*, *4*(3), 188–203. https://doi.org/10.1007/s10209-005-0005-9

German, K. (n.d.). *Look Back at CNET's Original iPhone Review.* Retrieved January 6, 2024, from https://www.cnet.com/tech/mobile/original-iphone-review/

Göransson, D. (2019, November 15). *What is a screen reader?* Axess Lab. https://axesslab.com/what-is-a-screen-reader/

Inclusive Design Research Centre. (n.d.). *Welcome to The Inclusive Design Guide.* The Inclusive Design Guide. https://guide.inclusivedesign.ca/

Joyce, A. (2022, January 30). *Inclusive Design.* Nielsen Norman Group. https://www.nngroup.com/articles/inclusive-design/

Khasnabis, C., Mirza, Z., & MacLachlan, M. (2015). Opening the GATE to inclusion for people with disabilities. *The Lancet*, *386*(10010), 2229–2230.

Koester, H. H., & Simpson, R. C. (2014). Method for enhancing text entry rate with single-switch scanning. *Journal of Rehabilitation Research and Development*, *51*(6), Article 6.

Koester, H. H., & Simpson, R. C. (2019). Effectiveness and usability of Scanning Wizard software: A tool for enhancing switch scanning. *Disability and Rehabilitation: Assistive Technology*, *14*(2), 161–171. https://doi.org/10.1080/17483107.2017.1406998

Lehmann, F., Kornecki, I., Buschek, D., & Feit, A. M. (2023). Typing Behavior is About More than Speed: Users' Strategies for Choosing Word Suggestions Despite Slower Typing Rates. *Proceedings of the ACM on Human-Computer Interaction*, *7*(MHCI), 1–26. https://doi.org/10.1145/3604276

Lesher, G. W., Moulton, B. J., & Higginbotham, D. J. (1998). Techniques for augmenting scanning communication. *Augmentative and Alternative Communication: AAC*, *14*(2), 81.

L'heureux, A., Grolinger, K., Elyamany, H. F., & Capretz, M. A. (2017). Machine learning with big data: Challenges and approaches. *Ieee Access*, *5*, 7776–7797.

Microsoft. (n.d.). *If you can move your head, you can move your world*. Microsoft. https://www.microsoft.com/buxtoncollection/a/pdf/HeadMaster%20Introduction.pdf

Monarch, R. M. (2021). *Human-in-the-Loop Machine Learning: Active learning and annotation for human-centered AI*. Simon and Schuster.

Morris, M. H., Santos, S. C., & Kuratko, D. F. (2021). The great divides in social entrepreneurship and where they lead us. *Small Business Economics*, *57*(3), 1089–1106. https://doi.org/10.1007/s11187-020-00318-y

Mystère, M. (n.d.). *English: Apple IIe with 2 Disk II drives and Apple Monitor II* [Graphic]. Own work. Retrieved January 6, 2024, from https://commons.wikimedia.org/wiki/File:Apple_IIe_%2B_Disk_II_drives_%2B_Apple_Monitor_II.JPG

My-T-Mouse software—On-screen keyboards, etc. (n.d.). Retrieved January 6, 2024, from https://www.specialneedscomputers.ca/index.php?l=product_detail&p=1149

Nam, S., & Fels, D. (2019). Simulation of Subjective Closed Captioning Quality Assessment Using Prediction Models. *International Journal of Semantic Computing*, *13*(01), 45–65.

Nam, S., Fels, D. I., & Chignell, M. H. (2020). Modeling closed captioning subjective quality assessment by deaf and hard of hearing viewers. *IEEE Transactions on Computational Social Systems*, *7*(3), 621–631.

Papastratis, I., Chatzikonstantinou, C., Konstantinidis, D., Dimitropoulos, K., & Daras, P. (2021). Artificial Intelligence Technologies for Sign Language. *Sensors (Basel, Switzerland)*, *21*(17), 5843. https://doi.org/10.3390/s21175843

Prenke-Romich. (2009). *Wivik Onscreen Keyboard*. https://file.prentrom.com/120/WiViK32NA.pdf

Quillsoft. (n.d.). *From Holland Bloorview to Berkeley Castle: The History of WordQ*. Quillsoft Ltd. Retrieved January 6, 2024, from https://www.quillsoft.ca/blog/wordq-history

Quinn, P., & Zhai, S. (2016). A Cost-Benefit Study of Text Entry Suggestion Interaction. *Proceedings of the 2016 CHI Conference on Human Factors in Computing Systems*, 83–88. https://doi.org/10.1145/2858036.2858305

Shane, S. A. (2008). *The illusions of entrepreneurship: The costly myths that entrepreneurs, investors, and policy makers live by*. Yale University Press. https://books.google.com/books?hl=en&lr=&id=clePgiDAoGQC&oi=fnd&pg=PR7&dq=what+are+investors+interested+in+for+start+ups&ots=P6EvtGDCR8&sig=PeHhLYOg1vBLe-KiSuJRN6-SNSU

Signapse AI | Breaking Barriers with our AI Sign Language Translator. (n.d.). Signapse. Retrieved October 2, 2023, from https://www.signapse.ai

Thomas, A. (1981). Communication devices for the nonvocal disabled. *Computer*, *14*(01), 25–30.

Todman, J. (2000). Rate and quality of conversations using a text-storage AAC system: Single-case training study. *Augmentative and Alternative Communication*, *16*(3), 164.

Todman, J., Alm, N., Higginbotham, J., & File, P. (2008). Whole Utterance Approaches in AAC. *Augmentative and Alternative Communication*, *24*(3), 235–254. https://doi.org/10.1080/08990220802388271

Trnka, K., Yarrington, D., McCaw, J., McCoy, K. F., & Pennington, C. (2007). The effects of word prediction on communication rate for AAC. *Human Language Technologies 2007: The Conference of the North American Chapter of the Association for Computational Linguistics; Companion Volume, Short Papers*, 173–176. https://aclanthology.org/N07-2044.pdf

Vanderheiden, G. (2022). A journey through early augmentative communication and computer access. *Journal of Rehabilitation Research and Development*, *39*(6), 39–53.

Web Content Accessibility Guidelines (WCAG) 2.1. (n.d.). Retrieved April 17, 2023, from https://www.w3.org/TR/WCAG21/

Conclusion and Final Remarks

Being an inclusive thinker, designer, innovator, educator and researcher requires constant consideration and reflection particularly if it is a new perspective or modus operandi. To embody the concept of inclusive thinking requires a broad as well as deep understanding of the variety of barriers, biases and circumstances that PWD face. This is a tall order for many people and it may not even be achievable in the short term.

There are numerous laws, regulations, standards, and organizational policies that apply to inclusion of and accessibility for PWD that can affect how researchers and instructors proceed. It is only a first step to have all of these rules in place. Another, often very difficult next step, is to expect that individuals are not only knowledgeable of these rules, standards and regulations, but also understand how to meaningfully apply them in their own teaching, design word and research. In addition, there are many abilities possessed by PWD and expecting to have knowledge and understanding of all of them can be a daunting task. However, relying on student services and others to do this work undermines embracing inclusive design principles and inclusive thinking.

As a result, it is vital that PWD are always part of the target user pool, and that from the beginning they are included in the work being done as much as possible as participant researchers and designers, students, advisors, mentors, and users. The hard part can be finding people who are interested in participating and contributing to the work, often as volunteers. Offering compensation can be incentivizing but not always as the work may not be of interest to an individual. While researchers may never be accepted in or become part of a community they are studying, it is important to meet and interact with individuals in that community by participating in events, attending social functions or even becoming a volunteer at relevant organizations. These efforts must also be sustained and not be just for one research project, or one person.

In this book, the reader has also been introduced to the concept of inclusive business using an overlay to the Business Canvas that is commonly used to describe a business model. Adding inclusion to a Business Canvas allows innovators, and individuals attempting to exploit their research and development to design their business inclusively from its

D. Fels et al., *Inclusive Design Premises, Policies, Protocols, and Practices: From Usability to Empowerment*, Synthesis Lectures on Technology and Health,
https://doi.org/10.1007/978-3-032-15746-1

inception. It also allows potential investors, board members, collaborators, employees, and potential customers to understand how inclusion is embedded into the planning and delivery of business products and/or services from the beginning. It may also offer unique opportunities for expanded markets, which may, in turn, be attractive to investors.

Throughout this book there are exercises and questions for reflection to stimulate inclusive thinking in readers. It is our hope that readers can go beyond the rules, regulations, standards, guidelines and letters of accommodation, and embrace inclusion and inclusive thinking in the many aspects of their education, training and work.

Appendix: Human-Centred Design

Human-centred design is a predecessor to Inclusive Design and has its roots in fields such as design, ergonomics, computer science and artificial intelligence. The echoes of this past can be noted in international standards such as ISO 9241-210 "Ergonomics of human-centred system interaction" (International Standards Organization 2019), which describes human-centred design as an "approach to systems design and development that aims to make interactive systems more usable by focusing on the use of the system and applying human factors/ergonomics and usability knowledge and techniques" (p. 2). ISO 9241-210 is defined by six specific characteristics:

1. The adoption of multidisciplinary skills and perspectives
2. Explicit understanding of users, tasks and environments
3. User-centred evaluation driven design
4. Consideration of the whole user experience
5. Involvement of users throughout design and development
6. Building and refining through an iterative process.

Such engineering-based approaches address the needs of the users of tools, since tools have predetermined functions. The difficulty in the case of consumer products, systems and services, is that the customer does not always adopt the point of view of a "user" of a "tool." As Gasson (2003) has highlighted, "user-centred system development methods fail to promote human interests because of a goal-directed focus on the closure of predetermined, technical problems" (p. 41). Designing for a "user" usually involves optimizing the characteristics of the product, system or service, based on a set of fixed preconceived cognitive plans and schemas. Such a view leads to designs which are efficient towards one or more predetermined usage patterns (Degani and Degani 2004) but, which are often characterised by only limited degrees of interactivity, exploration and learning.

References

Degani, A., & Degani, A. (2004). *Taming HAL: Designing Interfaces beyond 2001.* Springer.

Gasson, S. (2003). "Human-Centered vs. User-Centered Approaches to Information System Design." *Journal of Information Technology Theory and Application (JITTA)*, *5*(2), 5.

D. Fels et al., *Inclusive Design Premises, Policies, Protocols, and Practices: From Usability to Empowerment*, Synthesis Lectures on Technology and Health, https://doi.org/10.1007/978-3-032-15746-1

MIX
Papier aus verantwortungsvollen Quellen
Paper from responsible sources
FSC® C105338

If you have any concerns about our products,
you can contact us on
ProductSafety@springernature.com

In case Publisher is established outside the EU,
the EU authorized representative is:
Springer Nature Customer Service Center GmbH
Europaplatz 3, 69115 Heidelberg, Germany

Printed by Libri Plureos GmbH
in Hamburg, Germany